Social Media Marketing Made (Stupidly) Easy

The Ultimate, NO B.S. Guide to a
Social Media Strategy That Doesn't Suck

Vol.1 – Vol.5 of the Punk Rock Marketing Collection

By Michael Clarke
Publisher, Punk Rock Marketing

Printed in the United States of America

First Printing, 2014

Punk Rock Marketing

6912 Ohio Ave.

La Mesa, CA 91942

(310) 751-0343

PunkRockMarketing.com

To Jewyl,

for the love, for the support and for letting me give
cubicle life the middle finger

Table of Contents

About the Author

Michael Clarke is a former cubicle monkey and founder of Punk Rock Marketing Magazine, a publication devoted to helping small-business owners kick ass, make money and thoroughly rule the world.

He spends his days cursing Mark Zuckerberg and figuring out marketing shortcuts that help him — and small-business owners everywhere — avoid getting a "real" job.

How to Use This Book

Reading this book will NOT make you a "digital media expert" or a "social marketing guru."

You will NOT become a "thought leader" or grace the cover of WIRED.

You may not EVEN know enough to chair a "web 2.0" panel at the 2016 Eastern Delaware New Social Media Branding Conference-Palooza.

That's because: I don't even LIKE social media.

I believe:

☑ Facebook is a self-involved navel-gazing waste of time where 300 of my closest "friends" share every personal DETAIL about themselves.

☑ Twitter is a shallow, superficial metaphor for a world with ever-lowering attention spans and an OBSESSION with celebrities whose last name is Kardashian.

☑ YouTube is a weigh station for shut-ins and show-biz wannabes whose PRIMARY goal in life is to get "10K views on their YouTube video" and anonymously ridicule each other in fresh forms of comment torture.

And yet…

…social media is ALSO the quickest, cheapest and most effective way for small business folks to dominate their competition, turn casual customers into die-hard fans and survive the ups and downs of a world economy in turmoil.

Knowing the difference between the two is what this book is all about.

"Stand in the Place Where You Were"

While this book may not teach you much about "engagement" or "authenticity"...

It will walk you step-by-step through the LEAST you need to know to make this whole "social media thing" work for you. (And by work, I mean make you a metric crapload of money.)

You'll discover:

☑ A simple system for using Twitter to not only get your brand massive exposure, but also sell more of your product and services — without spending a single cent in advertising. (Part One — "Twitter Marketing That Doesn't Suck")

☑ A step-by-step process for creating brain-dead easy-to-make videos that help you conquer the ever-elusive top Google rankings — in a matter of a few weeks. (Part Two — "Video Marketing That Doesn't Suck")

☑ Strategies for turning strangers into fans and fans into customers — without breaking the budget on pointless, non-performing Facebook campaigns. (Part Three - "Facebook Marketing That Doesn't Suck")

☑ Insider secrets for turning pins into profits, using one of the hottest — if misunderstood — social networks around. (Part Four - "Pinterest Marketing That Doesn't Suck")

☑ A detailed — but easy-to-follow — blueprint for turning lukewarm email subscribers into fanatical, repeat customers. (Part Five - "Email Marketing That Doesn't Suck")

More importantly, you'll learn what NOT to do. (Because there's a helluva LOT not to do.)

"Now, for the Bad News..."

Spoiler alert: I do not cover EVERY single social network on the face of the Earth in this collection. I've only included strategies

I've actually used AND made money from. (Not just ninja hacks for how I got a few hundred retweets or upped my Klout score.)

If you're looking for extensive deep-dive looks at platforms such as Google Plus, LinkedIn, Instagram, Vine — or whatever shiny, new Internet venture some fresh-faced, Birkenstock-infused, Harvard dropout hipster just came up with — then let me suggest you check out the MANY social media guides on good, old Amazon. (There are a number of tomes. Some of them are even slightly non-sucky.)

But if you want to know what works — to find out what strategies will get you where you want to go without all that extraneous bullcrap — then give the strategies in this book a try.

I can't guarantee you'll get a Ph.D. in Social Media Studies, or that you'll acquire more Twitter followers than Lady Gaga…

But I do guarantee you'll learn a system for using Facebook, YouTube, Twitter, Pinterest — and even Email! — that can help you promote your brand, market your products and make a hell of a lot of money.

As Francine Jay said: "The goal is not to get more done, but to have less to do."

It's my goal that this book helps you do FAR LESS…and achieve WAY MORE than you ever thought possible.

Good luck! (And don't let all that social media bullcrap stand in your way.)

Michael Clarke
PunkRockMarketing.com
Michael@punkrockmarketing.com
Twitter: @punkrockbiz

TWITTER
MARKETING

THAT
DOESN'T SUCK

Vol.1
of the Punk Rock
Marketing
COLLECTION

Michael Clarke

Intro: A Beginner's Guide to a Very Strange Tool

Don't read this chapter.

Seriously.

If you're already using Twitter on a semi-regular basis and you're just looking for some ninja marketing techniques to move the needle on your business, you can SKIP this chapter.

You're busy. Ya got things to do. Like watch back episodes of "Law and Order." And make a frickin' living.

But if you're a Twitter newbie, who doesn't know their tweets from their Twitterati, then I want to tell you:

My 79-year-old aunt is on Twitter.

If SHE can work this micro-messaging service to devious and nefarious advantage, so can you.

The REAL learning curve on Twitter is deciphering what all that ridiculously-named terminology means.

So here is the briefest of brief overviews to help you get a B.A. in Twitter Studies and prepare you for the rest of our journey:

1. THE TWEET

This is the building block of Twitter. These are the short messages (140 characters max) that a Twitter user sends out via their status update feed.

Unless somebody "retweets" your tweet, or finds your tweet in a Twitter search, the only people who "see" your Tweets are your

Tweets can be almost anything: links to a website, a video, a blog post, a picture or simply whatever status update you'd like to share with your Twitter followers. ("Just had lunch with Lady Gaga. #NotImpressed.")

You can either send a tweet from your Twitter profile page — type in the status bar and hit "update" — or you can send a tweet from one of the many third-party Twitter dashboard tools available. (We'll go over these in a later chapter.)

2. The Retweet

This is the "I scratch your back, please, oh please, I beg you to scratch my back..." part of Twitter. This is where a Twitter user "shares" someone else's tweet with their own followers. (With the hope that the favor will be returned at some point.)

You can retweet anybody's tweet - your neighbor, Vladimir Putin, that strange man in the subway who talks to his bag of Oreos - meaning you don't have to follow them and they do not have to follow you in order for you to share their tweet with your followers.

The "how" of a retweet is pretty simple: You simply click the "retweet" button either on your Twitter page or on a third-party tool when viewing the tweet.

When you hit "retweet," it opens the tweet into a new field, with the symbol "RT" preceding your tweet. (This is how you can recognize a retweet from a regular tweet in your Twitter feed.)

The COOL part about retweets is that the person you retweeted is sent a copy of your tweet. (Helpful if you're trying to connect with a real Twitter heavyweight, such as Katy Perry or that moody teenage daughter of yours.)

You also get to throw in some editorializing before the original message, space permitting. (Editorializing and attitude are major pluses on Twitter.)

3. THE REPLY MESSAGE

I call this the "home invasion" of Twitter. This is where you send a message to someone on Twitter, by simply adding their Twitter handle (user name) with the @ symbol in front of it (Example: "Hey @Madonna, what's with the weird British accent?")

But this reply is not private, as all your followers will be sent a copy of your correspondence with the "Material Girl." So don't give away any national secrets here.

The cool ninja part of this action is that if the person replies to your reply— say @KimKardashian responds to your question about "What exactly is your talent, again?" — then all six million of Kim's followers will see the reply. (And you might pick up 1.7 million new Twitter followers/enemies in the process.)

4. THE DIRECT MESSAGE

This is like the "Early Bird Special" of Twitter. This is where you send somebody a PRIVATE message on Twitter. (The trick is, both of you have to be following each other to see the message.)

Sure, it's an option and it's something you CAN use with your more intimate Twitter friends, but most people don't use the DIRECT MESSAGE function.

Ever.

And...I don't really know how to say this politely...but sending a DIRECT MESSAGE is seen as a slightly uncool, old-fashioned, AARP way of doing things. (Reply messages and retweets are a much better way to go.)

One thing people often do is set up an automated system where each "new" follower gets an automated DIRECT MESSAGE thanking them for the follow and asking them to check out whatever crap they're promoting.

Don't do this. Nobody reads this crap. (And they tend to come off as spammy.)

5. THE HASHTAG

This might be the most misunderstood part of the Twitter ecosystem. This is where Twitter users add the # (pound) sign in their tweets followed by a specific phrase. (Example: #Kony2012, #DarkKnight, #RealHousewivesOfDenver, etc.)

Just remember to KILL the spaces in your hashtag term. (Writing #Dark Knight, is the same as writing #Dark.)

Because thousands of tweets are sent every nanosecond, hashtags can be a quick, effective way for your tweets to be discovered, in an otherwise congested Twitter highway. Generally, it's best to jump onto an existing hashtag bandwagon; the key is to find the right #hashtag.

#SelfPub and #SelfPublishing might appear the same to us fleshy humans, but in the Twitter-verse #SelfPub is the hands-down winner, in terms of number of tweets sent.

You CAN also create your own hashtag, to promote an upcoming special event, or to build interest in a cause you're trying to promote.

We'll go over hashtag best practices later, just know they're important. (And that most people royally screw them up.)

5. Twitter Lists

Twitter lists are a simple, but effective, way to organize the info in your Twitter feed.

You can organize lists by industry, customers, competitors or teenage miscreants who hope to date your daughter…whatever you want.

6. Twitter Favorites

This often overlooked feature allows users to "favorite" specific tweets.

And while it feels all warm and fuzzy when somebody "favorites" your own tweet, the real benefit comes from your ability to "favorite" tweets that specifically talk about your business. (For use as testimonials and reminders of how supremely awesome you are.)

It's like having a portable list of social proof that you can use to show how your customers connect with your business. (There are even tools that let you publish this info on your site.)

The Journey Begins…

So, that's about it. The rest you'll pick up as you go. This isn't brain surgery, though it may feel like it after reading the Twitter feed of somebody like Justin Bieber.

It's just a simple micro-messaging tool…that just so happened to have changed the world.

Chapter 1:

How to Make Money With Twitter

"Anyone who lives within their means suffers from a lack of imagination."

- Oscar Wilde

Ah, yes. Money.

How DO we make money with all this 140-character crap?

At the end of the day, "retweets and "engagement" and "followers" and TweetDeck and HootSuite and TwikiBoo...

...or whatever the hell new Twitter tool some Bay Area college dropout created in the basement of his parent's house are nice and make us feel super hip and cutting-edge....

...but they aren't nearly as important as the BIG question:

How do you **make money** *with Twitter?* (A question the founders of the company, and their investors, have been asking themselves for yezars.)

Really, I think it underlies an even bigger, more important question:

Which is:

How do I make sure I don't waste my time with Twitter?

I mean, it's nice to "engage" and "tweet" helpful links and interesting info...

…but how does that translate to actual money in the pocket?

So glad you asked…

"EXCUSE ME, WHILE I KISS THE SKY"

Don't worry, we're going to get into all the ninja tactics Twitter offers us as marketers. (And there are a ton of them. Some of them actually work.)

But let's talk BIG picture first.

There are essentially TWO ways to make money with Twitter:

THE DIRECT APPROACH

This is simple, and pretty straightforward: You "tweet" out a link through your Twitter account which asks for some action on the part of the person reading your tweet, which directly relates to income.

This could be:

- ☑ A link to a webinar you're running.
- ☑ A link to a sales page selling your latest widget.
- ☑ A link to a special event you're hosting.
- ☑ A link to a product or service you're an affilliate of.
- ☑ A link to a coupon or special offer.
- ☑ A link to a website squeeze page where you ask for an email opt-in. (Not sure what this is? We'll get to it later.)

Anything that pretty much asks people to go to some location and take action (so you can either sell them something or market to them in the future) is a DIRECT APPROACH to Twitter marketing.

And trust me, these DIRECT approaches work. (We'll go over in a later chapter just how to use them for top effectiveness.)

But they're a bit like eating chocolate cake. A little bit goes a long way.

And, sure, the idea of eating double-fudge brownie swirl all day long SOUNDS nice but, after a while, the law of diminishing returns kicks in and pretty soon your customers are left with a marketing bellyache.

THE INDIRECT APPROACH

This is a bit more subtle, and doesn't have the ROI (Return on Investment) that other forms of marketing do.

But, that doesn't mean it's not powerful. Because this is about presenting yourself as:

☑ An expert

☑ A cool person

☑ A compassionate business owner

☑ A problem solver

☑ Someone who is not a robot...

I would contend, it's the last one that is key.

I know all the "social media guides" tell you not to mix business with the personal.

But a quick TwitPic of your Jack Russell terrier chewing a pillow may do more for your marketing than all the coupons and free offers you can dream up.

And an honest tweet about something your company screwed up, and are working hard to rectify, can go a long way toward people seeing you as a trusted and humane company.

And not just somebody who's out for a quick buck. (Even if you ARE just out for a quick buck.)

"Get By With a Little Help From My Friends"

I started dabbling with social media for that most noble of reasons: I was TOO broke to afford "real" advertising.

And though I've gotten versed in all the latest social media gizmos, such as Facebook, YouTube, Pinterest and Tumblr...

Twitter is still the one I prefer. (And the one that tends to make me the most money.)

Because:

☑ The learning curve is low. (You just sign up and start tweeting away.)

☑ You can set it on autopilot, by setting up your tweets months in advance (No need to be awake for cool stuff to happen.)

☑ You can quickly see what works and what doesn't.

☑ You can quickly reach thought leaders (fancy word for smart people) and big dogs in your industry by simply tweeting/appealing to their vanity.

☑ There are tons, and I mean TONS, of tools to make it easy.

☑ My ADD-afflicted brain doesn't have the attention span for long conversations with people.

So whether you're a total social-media newbie or a hardcore Twitter veteran, I'm positive there's something in the Twitter universe that will help you directly, or indirectly, make money. (Which lets you buy more pillows for your Jack Russell.)

CHAPTER 1 KEY TAKEAWAYS:

☑ There are two ways to market through Twitter: DIRECT (sales pages, webinars, email opt-ins, affiliate offers, etc.) and INDIRECT (brand building, expert status, pics of your destructive canine, etc.).

☑ Twitter is PERFECT for social networking newbies and veterans alike. (It's easy and people don't get mortally offended if you try to promote something.)

☑ The author really likes Twitter because he has ADD and virtually no attention span.

Chapter 2:

3 Keys to a Kick-Ass Twitter Profile

"Not doing more than the average is what keeps the average down."

-William Lyon Phelps

We ain't gonna spend a ton of time on this.

Too many Twitter manuals go on and on about the need for a sleek, compelling background to your Twitter profile, or how your Twitter avatar needs to be "just right" before plunging into the deep waters of the Twitter-verse.

Uh...that may have been important back in the Mesozoic era (you know, way back in 2010), but today very few readers of your Twitter updates will actually see your tweets within your Twitter profile.

Most likely they'll consume them via a SmartPhone app or on some Twitter dashboard client like HootSuite or Tweet-Deck.

But there are THREE absolutely KEY AREAS you need to nail down when creating your profile before we start on your journey to Twitter awesomeness...

...and they will all go a long way toward ensuring your Twitter marketing success going forward.

Key No. 1: Pick a Name That Doesn't Suck

When you create your Twitter account, and verify the email connected to that account, you will be asked to come up with your Twitter name, or handle.

You will be tempted to use the name of your business or company. But here's the thing, if somebody retweets one of your tweets, your name will be included in that 140-character limit.

So, if you go with a Twitter name of @PetesPoolSupplyInc, that will gobble up precious Twitter real estate that could be better used in other areas.

And frankly, unless you're an instantly recognizable brand, then does anybody really get jazzed about the prospect of reading a tweet from @PetePoolSupplyInc? (You know, except for Pete.)

Instead, I would suggest coming up with a shorthand for describing your business, without sounding so frickin' corporate.

Like: @BBQBob, or @PoolPete, or @TheTaxKillers, or @VideoNinjas or @DenverAudio.

This also gives you the liberty of talking about a heck of a lot more than your boring day-to-day promo crap. (Trust me: Most everybody else finds our own business ventures exceedingly boring.)

And while there is a school of thought that Twitter handles should be personal names exclusively, I think using this biz shorthand can differentiate you from the pack.

If you DO want to use your personal name, and there can be some compelling reasons for this, PLEASE use a period to separate your first and last name:

Such as @michael.clarke

NOT

@michaelclarke

This will make it easier for readers to identify you in the hectic environment of the Twitter feed.

And if you're a big enough company, you may want to create separate Twitter handles for different areas of the biz. (Such as: @ShoeBarn, @AtlasHR, @LindsayLohanBailBonds, etc.)

KEY NO. 2: USE WHAT YOUR MAMA (AND THE TWITTER BIO) GAVE YA

So now ya got your profile name wrapped up, it's time to tackle one of the most important (yet neglected) parts of your entire Twitter marketing strategy.

Your Twitter bio.

You'd think people wouldn't spend time reading this stuff. You'd be wrong.

I'm constantly shocked how many leads and squeeze page opt-ins I get from this tiny little bit of real estate. (People are just nosy, I guess.)

The key, as with any aspect of social media, is to NOT be boring with your bio and give people a reason to head over to your website or opt-in page.

Here are five Twitter bio-creating tips:

1. **Use real words that humans use.** NOT "We are an Austin-based accountancy firm who provides structured tax solutions for individuals and businesses alike." Instead: "We're based in Austin. We like to save people money with taxes and stuff. Most of us majored in Math. (God knows why.)"

2. **Put a link in your bio if it's different from the main link in your profile.** You already are provided a space for a link to your site in your profile. No need to be repetitive and put a main site link in your bio…BUT if you want to di-

rect users somewhere else, such as a sales page or an opt-in page, then by all means do so here. (Just make sure it's a friendly URL, such as http://JimsAutomotive.com/ Deal…NOT…JimsAutomotive.com/site-Page4as90. aspf.) If you're not sure how to use "redirection" on your website to create a "friendly" URL, contact your local teenage computer hacker. (He/she can help you out.)

3. **You can CHANGE your bio whenever you want.** You aren't married to the bio you come up with when you create your profile. If you have a special deal, offer or product, be sure to change up your bio text to reflect the new stuff going on.

4. **You can add #Hashtags to your Twitter bio.** In a later chapter we'll go over the proper use of hashtags, but just know your bio is a good place to add common hashtags used in your industry. (Such as #CruiseVacations or #DogTraining.) Nobody does this. So doing so will make you stand out from the competition big time.

5. **Offers of FREE and discounted stuff do well, if done smartly.** You don't want to sound too sales-y in your bio, but something like "For your FREE copy of the 10 Biggest Plumbing Mistakes Homeowners Make eBook, head over to PlumbingPhoenix.com" would be appropriate.

Key No. 3: Filter Your Inbox

This isn't so much a Twitter profile hack as it is a way to avoid losing your frickin' mind. Because as anybody who uses Twitter knows, Twitter sends out more email than a Viagra spammer.

So, be sure to set up your email filters so that all email messages from Twitter are deleted that include the following phrases:

☑ "Favorited one of your tweets"

☑ "Do you know"

☑ "New follower"

☑ "Retweeted one of your tweets"

☑ "Check out your week on Twitter"

Doing this will help you stay productive - and avoid the Twitter sludge that can drag even the most organized inboxes down.

More importantly, it will help you focus on that most IMPORTANT form of Twitter correspondence of all: Real-life human beings who want to talk to you.

CHAPTER 2 KEY TAKEAWAYS:

☑ Choose a Twitter handle that sounds fun, but descriptive. (Avoid complex, dull-sounding corporate names.)

☑ Fill out your bio with key information about your company that doesn't sound like a press release.

☑ Feel free to change your bio to reflect your latest product or service you're offering.

☑ Links to FREE downloads, reports, videos or offers do really well.

☑ Add relevant hashtags to help your profile get discovered.

Chapter 3:

Yeah, But What the Hell Do I Tweet About?

"The secret of getting ahead is getting started."

-Mark Twain

Okay, so you've got a killer Twitter handle and your bio is optimized for marketing/cool person awesomeness.

Must mean you're ready to find those 2,500 Twitter followers who voraciously devour everything you tweet and send you thousands of dollars a month by buying your stuff!

Eh…not quite.

First, you've got to show a mix of Twitter activity before anybody will even consider following you. (And getting people to follow you is what this whole Twitter marketing thing is all about.)

I would shoot for at least 15 tweets before you try to get followers en masse. This will make you look less like a spammer, and more like a human being. (Which I hope you are.)

So what should those 15 tweets consist of?

Well, I think they should be as diverse as your regular Twitter activity going forward.

So, now is as good a time as any for me to introduce you to my: Ultimate Punk Rock Marketing Brain-Dead Tweet Formula!

These are the five areas of my Twitter portfolio that I stick to religiously. It's a breakdown of how I organize my tweets and schedule them throughout the week, in a variety of markets.

It doesn't matter whether you tweet 20 times a day or just once after lunch, follow this formula and you will be SURE that you are hitting all the important touchstones.

The Formula works like this:

☑ **20% of your tweets should be helpful, How-to Stuff.** This includes links to interesting blog posts, articles, industry-specific advice, the secret to why people watch the Kardashians, etc.

☑ **20% of your tweets should be Inspirational.** This includes inspirational quotes, motivating pictures, stories of courage, questions that people love to answer. (I know this may seem irrelevant to your industry. It's not! This stuff works like magic.)

☑ **20% of your tweets should be FUN.** These are funny videos, silly jokes, amusing questions, etc. (Bonus points if it has absolutely nothing to do with your industry.)

☑ **20% of your tweets should be Retweets.** Why constantly scour your brain for things to say when there are plenty of other people already saying interesting, funny, cool things that you can "borrow" and take credit for? (Just be absolutely sure you give attribution to the original tweeter.)

☑ **20% of your tweets should be Promotional.** This is stuff that directly boosts your bottom line. Such as: links to webinars, contests, opt-in offers, coupons, sales pages, etc. This is the DIRECT model of making money with Twitter marketing. (if this is done correctly it can be a very profitable part of your business.)

The BIGGEST problem most small biz folks make with Twitter is their balance of promo tweets is way too high. Trust me, any more than 20% and you'll really start to piss people off.

So what do you do if you want to send more promo stuff to your followers?

Simple…you send out more tweets.

I generally try to shoot for at least FIVE tweets a day, it makes it easier for me to break things up. that way (One tweet about how-to stuff, one tweet about fun stuff, etc.)

But start out slow and build gradually until you get the feel of it. In a later chapter, I'll show you some really cool automation tools that can make this a lot easier, but for now let me give you a few quick resources that can help you put all these tweets together.

TWEET AREA NO. 1: HELPFUL, HOW-TO STUFF

This could be almost anything:

- ☑ A video related to your industry that helps consumers with an issue they're having.
- ☑ An online article about some trend in your area of expertise (people just love trends; makes them feel smart).
- ☑ A blog post featuring a LIST of the top (whatever) that people absolutely need to know about (the only thing people love more than trends are numbered lists)

And where you find these reservoirs of kick-ass content will depend greatly on your business, but here are some go-to resources I never leave my Twitter home without:

Google Alerts: This is so simple, it's criminal. All you do is set up a Google Alert (http://google.com/alerts) based on a specific phrase, such as "pool care," and Google will email you the latest news articles, blog posts, and message-board ramblings around that subject. (Be careful, though. The alert will grab EVERYTHING. So if you put in "pool" you'll get articles about chlorine levels and pool sharks. So be careful!)

YouTube: There is a video about almost anything. (Don't believe me? Just search for "Japanese poodle fitness video" on YouTube (http://youtube.com) and you'll see what I mean.) So do a keyword search for your subject and share all the good helpful stuff you find. Just be sure to pick a video that has a majority of "likes" or "thumbs up." You don't want to share crap. (And there's a metric ton of crap on YouTube.)

AllTop: If you're not familiar with AllTop (http://alltop.com), then let me introduce you to your new Twitter best friend. This site is basically a blog aggregator (fancy word for collector of good stuff) broken out by subject. Not that extraordinary you say? Yeah, but this site employs humans, not robot algorithms. So you can bookmark the relevant page for your business and share the best human-endorsed stuff around.

The Big News Sites: I scour Yahoo (http://yahoo.com), New York Times (http://nytimes.com), and CNN (http://cnn.com) every once in a while to see if something interesting is happening. Most of them will even email you the most popular stories. (Hint: If it's popular for them, it'll probably be popular with your followers.)

StumbleUpon: I love this site because it's just so frickin' random. You can find ALMOST anything on StumbleUpon (http://stumbleupon.com). Photo blogs devoted to locations that look like James Bond villain hideouts. Interior designers imagining what TV show houses REALLY look like. An infographic showing you how to never pay a utility bill ever again. As long as you keep your interests relatively focused, you can find some amazing stuff here.

Tweet Area No. 2: Inspirational

If I'm being honest, inspirational quotes don't do much for me.

But I am in the vast Twitter minority.

Of all the kinds of tweets I've sent out over the years — in markets as diverse as self-publishing, real estate and even golf - by far the most retweeted, most shared and most downright "viral" have been quotes.

I think this is because of all the kinds of content floating in the world of social media they are so easily consumed...

You may not have time to read a blog post while you're checking your phone in the bathroom — and don't kid yourself, everybody does this — but who doesn't have time to read a single sentence?

And by "sharing" a quote it can make you look smart.

Or thoughtful. Or caring. Orz witty. Or whatever the hell other reason people love quotes.

And what kind of quotes do you share?

Well, I think this depends on your business. If you're running a restaurant, you'd want quotes about the joy of eating, drinking and being thoroughly merry. If you're a golf instructor you'll want to do things about maximizing your potential and not going insane while working on your short game.

I think no matter what your business, quotes that underscore some form of: "Life is Short; Appreciate What You Got; Be Your Best" are usually winners.

And where do you find choice tidbits of wisdom?

Well, you could do a simple search for "quotes" on the good old Google. But I prefer not to have to work that hard. (Or at all.)

I simply outsource it.

Two sites I highly recommend are oDesk (http://punkrock-marketing.com/odesk) and Elance (http://punkrockmarket-ing.com/elance). These are sites that help you find virtual assistants who, for a small fee, will do things such as collect quotes for your tweets…or even handle all of your Twitter duties.

When I NEED some quotes I simply create a posting and mention I'm looking for a Virtual Assistant to help me collect 200-400 quotes on a SPECIFIC TOPIC. (You gotta be specific!)

This can cost as little as $10-$15. (And it can make a huge difference to your business.)

Tweet Area No. 3: Fun Tweets

This is where a lot of business folks on Twitter really miss out. They forget that social media is SUPPOSED to be social. (Not a platform where you just hawk your wares.)

But sharing funny pictures, silly videos, random and crazy blog posts can be some of the best Twitter content to move the needle on your business. (And some of the most "shared" stuff you'll put out there in the Twitter-verse.)

Here are my go-to spots for fun Twitter material:

PopUrls: If you're looking for a way to waste your time, this site is it. PopUrls (http://popurls.com) pretty much aggregates EVERYTHING on the Internet. (Scary, huh?) I find most of my funny, weird gems here.

BuzzFeed: This is like PopUrls, but depending on the day, it can be a bit racier. (Which CAN be a good thing.) Whether it's the top porn search terms by country or the best soul-dancing photos, the random collection of weirdness that is

BuzzFeed (http://buzzfeed.com) has got it all.

The Onion: I'm an unabashed Onion (http://theonion.com) fan. I just love their satirical tone and their headlines are absolutely hysterical. (Perfect for this Twitter world we live in.) And some of them can actually be offensive. (Which works suprisingly well on Twitter.)

Funny or Die: Not everything on Funny or Die (http://funnyordie.com), the brainchild of Will Ferrell, is awesome. But most of it is, especially their in-house content. And funny videos do amazingly well in the TwitterSphere.

TWEET AREA NO. 4: RETWEETS

This one is pretty self-explanatory.

You just give a little bit of retweet love to somebody you're following on Twitter, and your followers get to enjoy the content as well.

Here are a few tips to ensure your retweets reach maximum effectiveness:

- ☑ **Retweet Twitter users whose followers you'd love to get access to.** If they reply or mention you, you'll get an added boost of promotion - and might pick up some more followers.

- ☑ **Retweet stuff that doesn't suck or hasn't been done to death.** Sharing the video of Susan Boyle singing "I Dreamed a Dream" might have been cool three years ago, alas, it is yesterday's news now.

- ☑ **Try to put a brief comment before the retweet.** Example: "You. Must. See. This. RT @jimmy.myers:…" This helps you put your own personality on things, and encourages people to follow you. (And not look like some noob jumping on the retweet bandwagon.)

☑ **Use Twitter lists to filter out the people worth retweeting**. We'll go over automation tools in a later chapter, but by simply creating Twitter lists, and adding high-profile users, it'll make it much easier to find the gold in the midst of all that Twitter crap.

TWEET AREA NO. 5: PROMOTIONAL

This is all you! This is stuff that can actually make you some serious money.

What you decide to promote here will depend on your business model. But here are a few best practices to ensure you get the most Twitter bang for your marketing buck:

☑ **Sales pages work better if they seem like content.** Saying "Check out the No.1 secret to dealing with hair loss" is better than "Get 50% off the hair loss solution that is sweeping the nation."

☑ **Discounts and offers work best for small purchases**. If you're selling something for under $15 or so, then feel free to pitch away.

☑ **Discounts and offers work even better for purchases that have a time constraint.** Limited-time offers and coupons with expirations work like magic. (And people will share them with their friends. Seriously.)

☑ **Ask for a retweet, if space allows.** People generally do what they're told, if they're told by someone they like. (And hopefully the other 80% of your tweets have made you someone they like.)

☑ **Links to free content that is an upsell in disguise works like MAGIC.** I love to tweet links to webinars or instructional videos or helpful blog posts…that actually turn out to be thinly-veiled sales pitches. They work really well, and they don't make people feel like you're a sleazy salesman. (Even if you are.)

CHAPTER 3 KEY TAKEAWAYS:

☑ Divide your tweets equally into FIVE different areas: 1) How-to 2) Quotes 3) Funny 4) Retweets 5) Promotional.

☑ Use YouTube, Google Alerts, AllTop and StumbleUpon to find the best helpful stuff to tweet.

☑ For quotes, either do a Google search or hire an outsourcer at a site like oDesk or Elance to help you out.

☑ When it comes to funny, The Onion, Funny or Die, Pop-Urls and BuzzFeed are fantastic resources.

☑ Set up a list of high-profile Twitter users and retweet their stuff in order to get access to their followers.

☑ Discounts and coupons work really well for your promo stuff. (As do free giveaways that opt people into a list.)

Chapter 4:

The Best (and Worst) Times to Tweet

"The early bird gets the worm, but the second mouse gets the cheese."

-Willie Nelson

This might be the most important chapter you read in this humble tome.

Because knowing WHEN to tweet is almost as important as knowing WHAT to tweet.

As somebody who has listened to all the webinars and read all the crappy blog posts, I know there's virtually NO CONSENSUS about the best time to tweet. (Some tell you weekends are best, some say weekends are for suckers, etc.)

So, I'll just give you what time periods have worked for me, over and over again. (And I've tested 'em all.)

If you feel my recommendations aren't right for you, feel free to tweak.

But in my experience these five principles can help you maximize your ability to market on Twitter, without wasting tons of time sending out tweets nobody sees. (Or wants to see.

Twitter Principle No. 1: Go Local or Global

What time you tweet will depend on what you're selling. If you're a local business, then time-zone considerations are relatively tight. (And will probably be during weekday business hours.)

But if you're peddling global software solutions, then you may want to stay flexible with your tweet times.

If you're looking for a hard-fast rule about tweet times, generally anything that hits the east coast of the United States in its Twitter sweet spot (more info on that in the next principle) is a good rule of thumb. (This is because the vast majority of online eyeballs is in the U.S. eastern seaboard.)

Twitter Principle No. 2: Mornings and Afternoons Are Golden

Sorry you night owls, but I find evenings pretty much comatose for Twitter response rates.

And, yes, there's less competition in the evenings, but so what? Sometimes there's less competition for a reason.

For me, the absolute best times to tweet are:

☑ 6:00 a.m. PST

☑ 7:30 a.m. PST

☑ 9:00 a.m. PST

☑ 10:30 a.m. PST

☑ 12:00 p.m. PST

This will all depend on what your business is and who you're trying to reach.

The big thing is: Don't tweet BEFORE 7:00 a.m or AFTER 5:00 p.m.

And before you worry that my suggested tweet times will force you to overtweet...don't worry! Your tweet will get lost in someone's feed so quickly that an hour and a half is plenty of time between tweets.

But five tweets a day may seem daunting at first. So, if you're looking for minimum amount when just staring out, you could do:

- ☑ 6:00 a.m PST
- ☑ 9:00 a.m. PST
- ☑ 12:00 p.m. PST

This is a decent way to break in, and will definitely get you a ton of traction with your followers. (Without losing your mind in the process.)

TWITTER PRINCIPLE NO. 3: FRIDAYS REALLY SUCK (ESPECIALLY IN THE AFTERNOON)

I'm not sure what happens on Fridays. Maybe the human brain starts the weekend early. (Or maybe it's those late-night "Burn Notice" reruns that turn our minds into mush.)

Whatever it is, Friday afternoons plain suck for Twitter engagement. I still tweet a bit on Friday morning, just to keep the old engine running, but it's definitely not where I put my primo content, or my heavy-duty promotional stuff. If you gotta choose, skip Fridays.

TWITTER PRINCIPLE NO. 4: MONDAYS ARE OKAY, BUT NOT IN THE MORNING

Ugh. Mondays.

Not only are they rough on your followers, who are getting back into the flow of work, but they're also pretty light on Twitter engagement, at least in the morning.

Unless of course you're trying to tap into that Monday escapist mindset.

Say you're a travel site offering vacation deals. Then Monday would be a fantastic day to tweet about that new Acapulco vacation package you got. (Especially if you operate out of Cleveland.)

Or if you've got a "Margarita Monday" special you're touting, then you could do a whole bunch of tweets related to curing the cubicle Monday blues.

This will depend on your business, but starting from the mindset of what your ideal customer is feeling and thinking, at that moment, is never a bad starting point.

TWITTER PRINCIPLE NO. 5: WEEKENDS ARE OKAY, BUT ONLY ON SUNDAY

I don't know what it is about Saturdays. But I have zero luck getting any real headway with my Saturday tweets.

I know you're different. I know you've got the secret sauce to reach people and break through the inertia. But I find most folks are too busy living lives to be on Twitter much.

Now, if you're someone who does a ton of business on Saturdays, like a pizza parlor owner or a realtor, then you'll want to jump on the Saturday Twitter train.

But for me, Sunday mornings and Sunday evenings are the best times to schedule your weekend tweets.

And by far, that 5-7 p.m. range on Sunday nights is just golden.

I don't know why, maybe after a long weekend with the family, the last thing we want to do is talk to humans who share our last name.

So, I usually schedule some kind of promotion on Sunday nights. (Engagement goes through the roof. And so do my sales.)

Twitter Principle No. 6: What the Hell Do I Know?

Again, what I advise may not be right for your business.

The quickest way to find out how utterly full of crap I am would be to test...and test and test...

Try out different times of day. Give Saturday a go. (Even though I know it won't work.) Tweet 47 times a day. Or only at 3:00 a.m.

See what excites your audience. (And if you do find something completely different, shoot me an email. I'd love to know what worked for you.)

But once you find your own secret sauce, don't deviate from your plan.

Once the plan is simple, successful, and repeatable, then you've got something you can scale. (And things you can scale, can usually make you money.)

CHAPTER 4   Key Takeaways:

☑ Determine if you need a global or local presence on Twitter. (If you're global, shoot for the east coast of America during the early morning and afternoon.)

☑ Weekday mornings and afternoons are awesome. (For starters: try to tweet at 6:00 a.m., 9:00 a.m. and 12:00 p.m. of your desired time zone during the week.)

☑ Skip Saturday. But don't forget Sunday evenings, 5-7 p.m. (Great engagement, and even greater profit potential.)

☑ Find your own system with constant tweaking and testing.

Chapter 5:

Art of the Perfect Tweet

"Have no fear of perfection
– you'll never reach it."

-Salvador Dali

We've talked a lot about what you should tweet out to your followers (don't worry, I'll soon show you how to get followers) and when is the best time to reach those people who hinge on every word you say.

But you may be asking what's the best way to organize a tweet? Should you use all 140 characters? And what's the best way to optimize your tweets for maximum marketing awesomeness?

So here are my tips to find that rare and elusive creature, the perfect tweet:

PERFECT TWEET TIP NO. 1: WRITE TWEETS THAT ARE 120-130 CHARACTERS

You've got 140 characters to work with. So why am I asking you to stop at 120?

Because you want to give people "room" to retweet you. If they give you some retweet love and you take up all 140 characters with your rambling, then they have to "edit" to include username to get the retweet out there.

And as anybody in business will tell you, if you ask people to do anything above the bare minimum, they probably won't do it. So keep those tweets short and enjoy the bounty of retweet awesomeness.

Perfect Tweet Tip No. 2: Write Tweets Shorter Than 100 Characters If You Can

This one shocked me. But according to Buddy Media, tweets less than 100 characters boast a 17% boost in engagement. (I'm not sure how they define "engagement," but I'm pretty sure it's better than "non-engagement.")

So, if possible, keep your tweets short. (It'll make your tweets stand out from the usual crap.)

Perfect Tweet Tip No. 3: Place Your Link 25% of the Way Into the Tweet

According to social media savant Dan Zarrella over at HubSpot (http://hubspot.com) the highest engagement on Twitter comes from tweets with links approximately a quarter of the way into the tweet.

So…

"Apocalypse is near: http://bitly.463 Michael Bay to remake Mutant Ninja Turtles"

…is better than:

"Apocalypse is near. Michael Bay to remake Mutant Ninja Turtles: http://bitly.463"

I have no idea why. And I don't care. It's worked for me, and it'll work for you.

Perfect Tweet Tip No. 4: Kill the Passive Voice and Use Active Verbs

Twitter is like poetry. Ya gotta be tight and economical with your words. So, this wouldn't be super awesome:

"We are presenting a webinar later this afternoon, where we will be discussing the merits of Twitter marketing http://bit.ly/twitter"

But this would be a helluva lot better:

"Crush your competition with Twitter. Find out how in this kick-ass webinar TODAY: http://bit.ly/Twitter"

Perfect Tweet Tip No. 5: Don't Forget Them Hashtags

Have to be honest. For the longest time I never used hashtags. (Just didn't understand their appeal.)

Well, was I a total moron.

People just love 'em and they can help get your tweets discovered rapidly.

There are three basic ways to use hashtags:

a. **Group your tweets within an existing hashtag category,** such as #asklochte; #writerquotes; #thingsgirlsdo; #tweet-event. The best place to find this info is at Hashtags.org (http://hashtags.org) and leverage the work somebody else has already done.

b. **Create your own hashtag to brand your event, company or special offer.** This is quite powerful and done best when it's funny or witty. But be sure to research your hashtag first, before using. (The dessert company Entenmann's got in trouble for using the hashtag #notguilty at the same time supporters of murder suspect Casey Anthony were also using #notguilty. Yeah, that's awkward.)

c. **Use a hashtag ironically,** such as #NoMoreShaveTech or #WhatWouldMichaelBayDo. This one may not have an immediate marketing benefit, but it can make you seem funny, articulate and somewhat human.

Perfect Tweet Tip No. 6: Try to Use a Real Hyperlink (If Possible)

If you're using any kind of automated Twitter service, such as TweetDeck or HootSuite, they'll usually offer some form of link shortening service.

Don't do it. (If you can.)

Putting a "real" hyperlink — http:yoursite.com/coupon as opposed to http://bit.ly/78$#2 — will boost your click-thru rates and help put more moolah in your pocket.

Perfect Tweet Tip No. 7: Use Interesting Characters to Stand Out

Anything that helps your tweets stand out is a good thing, far as I'm concerned. And I do mean anything.

I love the tilde… (~)

It's just so weird and can convey, well, whatever the hell I want it to convey.

Colons (:) are also good right before a hyperlink.

As are any variety of characters: ($, %, ^, *, &)

And even ALL CAPS can be effective. (Just don't go overboard.)

And if you are going to feature a blog, video, or picture then do the following before the link:

[BLOG]

[VIDEO]

[PIC]

It'll help boost click-thru rates. (Not to mention help those ADD-inflicted Twitter users - and I'm one of those - quickly scan your Twitter output for what they REALLY want.

CHAPTER 5 KEY TAKEAWAYS:

- ☑ Keep your tweets between 120-130 characters to allow easy retweet-ability.

- ☑ Keep your tweets below 100 characters for maximum engagement.

- ☑ Put your link a quarter of the way into your tweet.

- ☑ Get to the point. Use verbs. Skip adverbs.

- ☑ Use hashtags to promote your special event or brand. (Be sure to check nobody is using the tag.)

- ☑ Use real links (if you can.)

- ☑ Use interesting characters to make your tweets stand out.

Chapter 6:

How to Get a Million Followers in 24 Hours

"To handle yourself, use your head; to handle others, use your heart."

-Eleanor Roosevelt

Okay, so maybe a MILLION followers is a bit optimistic - but 500K for sure. :)

Seriously, though, we have come to the most CRUCIAL yet MISUNDERSTOOD part of Twitter marketing.

And that is: How to get some frickin' followers who can eventually turn into customers who eventually put money in your pocket.

I have to warn you though, this section is not for the timid.

If you don't like to offend or step on toes, then the techniques outlined here may not be for you.

But if you want to get a ton of Twitter followers quickly (but not so fast as to raise any red flags with the Twitter gods), then these tips will be right up your marketing alley.

So, here are my THREE Totally Ninja Techniques for Getting a Buttload of Twitter Followers Fast:

Ninja Technique No. 1: Follow to Be Followed

I know what most of the gurus tell you.

Mass following people on Twitter is spammy. And it's un-ethical. And it makes you look like a huckster.

Yeah, and it totally works. (If you do it right.)

The key is to have a plan, and work that plan consistently. (And without all those crappy mass-follow automated solutions that seem to spring up every week.)

So, here's what I do with every new Twitter account I've created and it's worked EVERY single time.

1. **Find your tribe.** Choose 15-20 "big-time" Twitter users (at least 2K followers) whose followers represent your ideal customer. (Could be a competitor, a local celebrity, your favorite chef, the President of Denmark, etc.)

2. **Schedule three "following" sessions a week.** My ideal following times are Tuesday 12 p.m., Thursday 12 p.m., and Sunday 5 p.m. But you can do it whenever you like. (Just avoid Saturdays and late evenings.)

3. **For each session, follow the most recently active followers of 3-5 users on your big-time user list.** This is easy to do. Just find the Twitter profile page of the big-time user, click on the followers link and start following away.

4. **Try NOT to follow companies or people without profile pictures and written bios.** Unless you're on the B2B (Business-to-Business) train, you're not interested in other businesses. While people without pictures aren't frequent users. (And folks without bios are usually Russian hackers. Or maybe it's just me.)

5. **Give the people you just followed TWO FULL DAYS to follow you back, and then unfollow folks who didn't fol-**

low you back. Generally about 40% of everybody I follow will follow me back. (Not always, but it's a general rule.) It's vital you give people a full two days, otherwise you'll be seen as a spammer and Twitter can close down your account quicker than a Kardashian marriage.

6. **Go slow.** Twitter has a limit of how many people you can follow in a given time. (The maximum follow limit is approximately 10% more than the number of people who follow you.) But don't worry, stick with it and before you know it, you'll find yourself building a decent following in no time.

Ninja Technique No. 2: Put Twitter Buttons Everywhere!

The first technique, by far, is the one where I see the quickest gains.

But it's this second technique - in which you place a "follow me on Twitter icon" in specific areas of your internet footprint - that I see the most lasting and permanent Twitter connections.

That's because these are people who already have some kind of affinity with me and want to know what else I'm up to.

And people like that make for great Twitter marketing buddies.

The HOW is pretty simple: just head over to the Twitter Button Resource page (http://punkrockmarketing.com/twitterbutton) and grab some code for your blog or website.

It's the WHERE that most people screw up. So here are my favorite (yet often overlooked) places where to put Twitter icons to boost my follower count:

☑ **Email.** Total no-brainer here, but I'm surprised how many people don't take advantage of the real estate at the bottom of their email newsletters or info blasts that encourage people to follow them on Twitter.

☑ **Your website.** Here's another lost opportunity for many marketers. Most online newbies sure know how to cram a bunch of crap on their website...except for stuff that actually lets them continue to market to their customers. Don't forget to throw a twitter icon in your website navigation so the conversation never ends.

☑ **Blog posts and articles.** If you do any kind of written website content, it's crucial you have some kind of "follow what I'm doin' on Twitter" nearby. (Especially if you're guest posting.)

☑ **Video.** If you do have any kind of video or YouTube presence (and you damn well should), then putting your Twitter info can be invaluable here. (And will usually get some easy retweets for your videos along the way.)

☑ **Flyers/Print Materials**. If you do have any kind of direct marketing be sure to include your Twitter handle. Give people a reason to follow, such as "Find out about our specials." (Not just: "Please follow me so I can make my car payment.")

☑ **Your Front Counter.** If you're a brick-and-mortar business, you're absolutely brain dead if you don't have some kind of thing-y at the front counter encouraging people to follow you on Twitter. Again, you gotta give 'em an incentive. Free, cheap stuff is usually good.

☑ **Your body**. I have a client who puts his Twitter handle, along with an offer of a free coupon, on his company-issued sandwich shop t-shirts. Twitter followers went up 300%! (Mostly from people standing in line to buy sandwiches.)

NINJA TECHNIQUE NO. 3: ANSWER PEOPLE'S QUESTIONS

Don't think I'm breaking any news when I say good business is about helping people solve problems.

But for some businesses this can be difficult. It can be hard to find people BEFORE they really NEED you. (Such as a personal injury lawyer. Or a Justin Bieber life coach.)

But Twitter is perfect for jumping into the confused and muddled vortex your prospective customers find themselves in, and deliver kick-ass solutions. (And all without chasing a single ambulance.)

So how do you find people who need your help? Here's the system I use:

- ☑ **Go to Twitter advanced search.** (http://twitter.com/search-advanced)

- ☑ **Add your industry-specific keywords.** In the "All of These Words" field put in your keyword (such as "sandwich" or "pool cleaner" or "dry cleaner") and a "?" (No quotes)

- ☑ **Strip out the spammers.** In the "None of These Words" field, put in the phrase "http" (no quotes). That will remove all the auto-posters (robots).

- ☑ **Add the question words.** In the "Any of These Words" field put in "recommend," "how," "find"…or whatever words you think might fit your particular field. (No quotes)

- ☑ **If you're a local business, specify your area.** In the "Places" field put in your town or city.

- ☑ **Hit Search.**

- ☑ **Look for questions you can answer.** Be cool. Don't be sales-y. Just answer questions like a human being.

Trust me, do this for a little while and you'll be shocked how quickly you can grow a dedicated following. (Who just so happens to give you money.)

Social media expert Gary Vaynerchuk built an entire winemaking empire - not to mention a lucrative speaking career - by simply answering people's questions about vino. You could do worse than follow his lead.

CHAPTER 6   KEY TAKEAWAYS:

☑ Follow the followers of big-time users in your industry to build up your Twitter following.

☑ Be sure to give people you recently followed at least two days to follow you back. Shoot for three following sessions a week.

☑ Put your Follow Me on Twitter icons everywhere (including email signatures, newsletters, store counters, your employees, etc.)

☑ Answer questions (with the Twitter question search above) to help people out, and add people to your Twitter following.

Chapter 7:

Contests, TweetChats and Live Streams...Oh My!

"If you're not gonna go all the way, why go at all?"

-Joe Namath

So, at this point, you pretty much have a Master's Degree in Twitter Studies.

I think it's safe to say that with the knowledge you've consumed so far, you know more than nearly 95% of all business peeps when it comes to Twitter marketing.

But now it's time to get a full-on Ph.D. in Twitternomics. (Without all the crippling student loan debt.)

Because no matter how many followers, retweets or "engagement" you have, it doesn't mean a damn thing until you can translate that Twitter activity into paying customers.

And there may be no better form of social media marketing than Twitter for converting browsers into buyers. So, here are a couple of out-of-the-box, profit-generatin' techniques that have worked really well for me:

SUPER NINJA TWITTER TRICK NO. 1: TWITTER CONTESTS

Want to build your Twitter following and customer base fast? Throw a Twitter contest.

People love to win free stuff. And the stuff doesn't even have to be that amazing.

I'm constantly amazed at the FREE crap people scurry around trying to win on Twitter. (Imagine what would happen if you actually gave away something decent.)

Here's how to organize your very own Twitter contest:

1. **Decide on a prize that doesn't totally suck.** Could be an iPod. Dinner for two at your restaurant. A free one-hour consultation in your office. A date with Brad Pitt. Whatever.

2. **Create a special website landing page with details about the contest.** This could be on your blog, your website, etc. Just so long as it's a link. (Make sure to have a picture of the prize that doesn't suck.)

3. **Shorten that special website landing page URL.** You could use a site like Bit.ly (http://bitly.com) or TinyUrl (http://tinyurl.com). Just create a shortened version of the landing page address. (Example: http://bitly/8&*2)

4. **On your contest detail page let people know how they can win the special something you're giving way.** Generally you'd want them to follow you on Twitter and tweet out something like: "Just entered to win a FREE iPod. Follow @punkmarketing and retweet http://bit.ly/8&*2 #Freepunkstuff (The unique hashtag is key. This will let you track entrants into the contest. Don't forget to come up with an original #hashtag that nobody else is using.)

5. **Promote the contest everywhere.** On Twitter, Facebook, YouTube, the side of your teenage daughter's car, etc.

6. **Allow the contest to run for about 4-7 days.** This will depend on your audience, but I generally like to keep my contests within that timeframe. (Anything longer than a week tends to sap effectiveness.)

7. **Pick a winner.** Use the hashtag search in Twitter search (http://twitter.com/search-home) or Bing Social search (http://www.bing.com/social) to find a list of all the people who retweeted your tweet.

8. **Announce the winner...everywhere.** Again on Twitter, Facebook, YouTube, etc.

9. **Wait 6 months, then do it again.**

SUPER NINJA TWITTER TRICK NO. 2: TWITTER Q&A

The problem with Twitter contests is you get a lot of freebie seekers.

Which is okay. To a point. But ideally you'd like people to give you hard currency for your efforts. And that's why I really like Twitter Q&A's.

The leads I've gotten from Twitter Chats tend to be much higher than from Twitter contests. (Even if the overall numbers are slightly lower.)

And by riffing on your area of expertise, you not only put a face to your business, but you become the go-to person — in your follower's mind — for your given industry.

Trust me: it's like holding your very own 30 minute infomercial, without the bad lighting and overpriced blenders.

So here's how you run a Twitter Q&A:

1. **Pick a hashtag.** This is important. You will be using this to not only promote the event, but also keep track of who's attending. Make it unique and make it somewhat not sucky. (#AskJim or #AskCompanyName would be good ways to go.)

2. **Schedule a time for the chat.** I think the sweet spot is anywhere from 30-45 minutes, though I've seen people go as long as 90 minutes. (Not something my ADD can handle, but if you can, knock yourself out.)

3. **Promote the event with the hashtag.** This is key. You gotta get the word out about your event. So make sure everything you've got — your website, blog, Facebook page, Twitter account, back of your car — has the hashtag and topic you plan to talk about.

4. **Tweet about it constantly.** This is a no-brainer, but still… many small-biz types miss out on this. You gotta let people know what you're doing. (Don't forget the #hashtag.)

5. **Write a press release.** If you think your chat isn't important enough to do a press release, then you should see the crap people write press releases about. Believe me, if you're answering questions in your knowledge wheelhouse, it's worth a press release. (And you can really get the word out. Not to mention help your Google rankings.)

6. **Do the Chat.** Here's how it works: When the event starts, send out a tweet letting folks know to ask questions using the designated hashtag. Then retweet their question, so people see it and then answer with another tweet. Su-per simple.

7. **Wrap up the chat with a call to action.** Thank everybody for attending and let them know if they've got more questions, or they want to get a copy of whatever free thing you're peddling, then they can reach you at your website. (Be ready to have some way to collect their info. Because they are now hot leads.)

Here's the thing, no matter what business you're in, you have some level of expertise that civilians/possible customers might find interesting. (And Twitter chats are fantastic ways to share that expertise.)

Super Ninja Twitter Trick No. 3: Live Twitter Video

I know what you're saying. Yeah, but streaming video doesn't have a place in my marketing.

That's what I thought. Until I did it. And now, I'm only sad I didn't do it earlier.

Whether you're recording a live event or talking from the comfort of your own double-wide trailer, live video on Twitter can do some amazing things for your marketing.

Here are two truths I know for sure:

a. Most of us are walking around with smartphones that have better HD video recording capabilities than camcorders did a mere three years ago.

b. People LOVE video. (Even if it's not really of anything that interesting.)

One of the best tools for broadcasting live video on Twitter is TwitCam (http://twitcam.livestream.com). With the Twit-Cam Live Stream function you simply:

☑ Connect your webcam

☑ Login to Twitter

☑ Hit the broadcast button.

Best of all, they take care of the link that people follow to see your video. (And they'll host the video in their archive afterwards. Not too shabby.)

I've had clients as diverse as surf-school instructors, caterers and even dentists do these from a variety of locations.

And again, something about video makes people "trust" you. (Even when you shouldn't be trusted.)

My only BIG TIP would be: make sure you've got a good microphone. (In video, audio is WAY more important than video. Weird, but true.)

CHAPTER 7   KEY TAKEAWAYS:

☑ Throw a Twitter contest by asking entrants to retweet a designated message. Be sure to use a special #hashtag to track results.

☑ Plan a Twitter Q&A where you can answer questions from folks. Don't forget to send out a press release to promote the event.

☑ Do a high-tech Q&A with Twitter Live Video Streaming. Use TwitCam, or another similar service to reach the masses with your smartphone.

Chapter 8:

Setting It All on AutoPilot

"The first problem for us all, is not to learn, but to unlearn."

-Gloria Steinem

The beauty, and I mean the absolute beauty, of Twitter is that like those cheesy rotisserie grill infomercials…

You can "set it and forget it."

It's possible, if you've got enough content and quotes and funny videos and promotional links stored up, that you can schedule your Twitter activity months, if not years, in advance.

This is because (unlike other social platforms like Facebook, Pinterest and Instagram) Twitter has what techie types call an "open API" - which is a fancy way of letting developer-types grab their data and create cool toys to make your Twitter life easier.

Now, not all Twitter tools are created equal. (In fact, some of the third-party tools' names are as dumb as the tools themselves.)

But there are a few I can't live without. And while most of them have a free version, premium versions can make your life much easier. (When you're starting out, just grab the FREE tools and give 'em a test drive.)

Twitter AutoPilot Tool No. 1: HootSuite

I believe the official term for HootSuite is that it's a dashboard client for Twitter.

To me, it's just a kick-ass way to use Twitter, and is pretty much my absolute number one social media tool I use everyday.

Why?

HootSuite lets you feed multiple Twitter streams into one single dashboard. Meaning, if you've got multiple Twitter accounts, you can handle all of the scheduling, commenting, retweeting, replying, and favoriting in one place.

But, wait! That's not all! (Cue the music.)

These streams can almost anything: LinkedIn Groups, Facebook profiles, Twitter searches, Twitter lists, Facebook pages…

So you can pretty much handle all your social media goodness in one place.

The FREE version lets you sync up to five twitter accounts, which is perfect for most businesses. The PRO version comes with 50, and up to 100 at an additional cost.

You also get a fair amount of analytics, so you can track what works and what doesn't. (To check it out, head over to http://punkrockmarketing.com/hootsuite.)

Alternatives include: TweetDeck (http://punkrockmarketing.com/tweetdeck), SocialOomph (http://punkrockmarketing.com/socialoomph) and a bunch of other crappy tools I can't stand. For my vote, HootSuite is still the best.

Twitter AutoPilot Tool No. 2: Friend or Follow

The manual labor of having to "unfollow" masses of people in the quest to build up your Twitter fan base can be quite daunting.

But with Friend or Follow (http://friendorfollow.com) it's a breeze.

All you do is sign up and import your Twitter account, and then the tool shows you which of your followers doesn't follow you back.

Then it's just a matter of clicking "Select All" and hit unfollow. Super, super easy.

TWITTER AUTOPILOT TOOL NO. 3: TWELLOW

Told you these names were ridiculous.

But as silly as Twellow (http://twellow.com) sounds, it's actually a pretty cool tool. Because Twellow lets you find people based on keywords AND locations. (Effective for local and global businesses alike.)

The search can be a little funky; it's based on biographical data. But for a FREE tool, it's absolutely amazing. (And I've padded my bank account considerably using this tool.)

There are some other alternatives out there, but nothing I can think of that's quite as good.

TWITTER AUTOPILOT TOOL NO. 4: A BUNCH OF OTHER COOL/CRAZY TOOLS

There are some other really neat Twitter automation tools I like, but don't use day in and day out.

Clicktotweet (http://clicktotweet.com) is a really simple way to promote your stuff by letting people click a button and which automatically updates their Tweet status with a pre-populated tweet promoting your marketing goodness.

Twtqpon.com (http://twtqpon.com) is probably the best of the bunch, as it allows you to create an online coupon code that your readers can redeem. It's a very cool way to spread the word (and the profits.)

CHAPTER 8 KEY TAKEAWAYS:

☑ Use tools like HootSuite or SocialOomph to manage ALL your social media activity. (And schedule your tweets weeks in advance.)

☑ Rely on the ever-reliable Friend or Follow to help you build up your Twitter rapidly. (By getting rid of Twitter deadweight.)

☑ Use Twellow to find users who match your ideal customer interests and locations.

☑ Explore tools like ClicktoTweet and Twtqpon to automate some serious money-making Twitter marketing efforts.

Epilogue:
This Wasn't Supposed to Happen

Twitter, like most technological innovations, was an accident. (And was never intended to be anything but a side project for the guys working on it.)

It started off as a simple micro-messaging service that helped colleagues keep in contact during the workday. (The reason for the 140-character limit was based on SMS cell phone limits and had nothing to do with the relative merits of a super-short tweet length.)

Ev Williams and Biz Stone, the founders of Twitter, certainly couldn't have predicted they would create a technology platform that would change the way we write, read, communicate and live.

But they did.

And today, Twitter is used just as much by bored suburban teenagers who desperately want to be vampires as it is by students in the Arab world dreaming of a new life.

And that's the mind-boggling part of Twitter.

Messages can spread in a matter of seconds to thousands of people you will never meet.

And unlike platforms such as Facebook or LinkedIn, Twitter isn't about getting membership into an exclusive club or building your "network of friends."

It's about breaking down the doors of the club and finding out if your message resonates with the world.

Now, it's possible you won't be sending out tweets that bring down a fascist regime.

But...

Every once in a while you will send out something that spreads like wildfire. (I sent out a tweet about my mom's chemotherapy struggles that got 1,300 retweets and some amazingly personal emails.)

So, as you plan you Twitter marketing calendar, just remember we all like to buy stuff from people we like and trust.

And people who remind us, in a simple way, how important it is to stay upbeat, strong and committed to what we want don't come off as marketers.

They come off as people we like and trust.

Here's hoping the tips in this book help you become the trustworthy and likable Twitter ninja I know you can be.

*   *   *

Terrified of Twitter? Don't worry!

Grab your very own **FREE Twitter Marketing Cheat Sheet,** by heading over to **PunkRockMarketing.com** TO-DAY and get instant access to your very own Twitter Marketing Checklist.

It's so easy, Lady Gaga can do it without a costume change!

Again, head over to **PunkRockMarketing.com** TODAY and get your **FREE Twitter Marketing Cheat Shee**t.

And if you have any questions, just drop me a line at Michael@punkrockmarketing.com.

Okay...now you're ready for...

Vol.2
of the Punk Rock
Marketing
COLLECTION

VIDEO
MARKETING
THAT
DOESN'T SUCK

Michael Clarke

Prologue:
Why You're a Total F$#*$ Moron If You Don't Do Video

I remember the first time I heard the phrase, "THIS is the YEAR you MUST do Video."

That was 2009. (Pretty sure I made a note of it in my Blackberry Curve 8300.)

Since then, it seems, every nanosecond some rambling pundit, like myself, comes out with their predictions about how THIS is the year video will dominate everything...

...and how any small business owner who doesn't RIGHT NOW, THIS VERY MINUTE drop everything they're doing and pick up a video camera and start creating 45 YouTube videos...

...is going to fall into bankruptcy, lose their livelihood and wander the streets in a disoriented post-marketing stupor.

No wonder most business owners get a bit punch-drunk when they hear that constant video marketing refrain.

Truth is: RIGHT NOW does represent an absolute, goldmine opportunity for marketers to start doing video.

Because creating, promoting and distributing your videos has NEVER been easier.

The best part: YOUR customers don't know that.

Most people are impressed by the fact it took you all of THREE MINUTES to talk to an electronic device with a blinking light...

...and then spent SEVEN MINUTES to cut out the boring parts where you forgot to turn the camera off...

...and then dedicated a monumental THIRTY SECONDS to upload the video and give it a title that wasn't totally pointless.

"Just Give Me a Reason, Just a Little Bit's Enough"

So, before we jump into the nuts-and-bolts of video marketing (and there are quite a few of them), here are a few major-league kick-ass reasons why video marketing is not only an effective and rather inexpensive way to market to new customers...but a revolutionary way to do business.

Kick-Ass Reason No. 1: Video is Cheap

But what about all that gear? And that expensive editing software and all the time it takes to memorize aspect ratios and HD video export formats?

Relax. Breathe.

Yes, there MIGHT be a bit of an initial investment in some gear. (But if ya got a smartphone, that expense can be greatly minimized.)

But when it comes to managing your marketing costs — namely trying to get a ton of leads without taking out a second mortgage — video is the MOST effective and CHEAPEST form of marketing there is.

Just TRY to get on the first page of Google with an article

on your website, or even worse, some clumsy Google PPC campaign.

And while you're waiting six months for Google to index your blog post or paying $7.50/click on some ultra-spendy Google Adwords campaign, I can rip off a quick video and get my video on the first page of the search engines in a matter of a week. At nearly 10% of the cost. (That's about as kick-ass as it gets.)

KICK-ASS REASON NO. 2: VIDEO IS FAST

While you're spending two hours on that 400-word opus that Google may or may not rank you for…

…I can create ten videos and have my entire video editorial calendar wrapped up for the next two and a half months.

And I say this as a guy whose entire job years ago was writing website content.

I love writing. (I'm one of those hopeless English Majors who actually read, and liked, "Moby Dick.")

But written text online moves at GLACIAL speed compared to video.

And, let's be honest, when was the last time you actually READ an entire 400-word anything online. (Yeah, that's what I thought.)

KICK-ASS REASON NO. 3: VIDEO GETS SHARED… A LOT!

Know what gets shared the most on Facebook? Pictures of friends AND videos.

So if you're looking to boost business at your burger joint, instead of pouring thousands of dollars into offline print marketing or PPC campaigns that have crappy ROIs…

...instead, just make a funny behind-the-scenes video of your kitchen crew, and you'll get a much bigger bang for your marketing buck.

Reason No. 4: Video Puts a (Human) Face to Your Business

All those pages of snappy sales copy and reams of direct-mail pieces won't make people feel nearly as connected and interested in you, and your business, as video.

I could tell you it's because 90% of our judgments are based on what we can see. (Though that might be part of it.)

I think the real reason is that video, by the medium's nature, "feels" intimate and personal.

I can't tell you how many emails I've gotten from people who saw one of my vids, and felt like they just already "knew" me. (Kinda stalker-ish. But, good, if you're in the marketing biz.)

And if you approach your video marketing with a sense of humor, and a willingness to look slightly foolish on camera, there's NOTHING that can stop you.

Kick-Ass Reason No. 5: Video can help you own your market

I can't tell you how many times I've entered into a market where there's some long-time, old-school established competition...

...and blown them away in just a matter of a few weeks with three or four strategic videos.

That's because videos give you instant credibility. And help differentiate you as a big fish in a super-sized pond.

Because if most businesses do dip their toe into video marketing, they usually suck at it. And, most people are lazy and don't want to read anything more than a paragraph.

But give 'em a couple two-minute videos and they'll be putty in your hands.

And you can sell a whole lot of crap to putty.

Chapter 1:

Which Kind of Video Should I Do?

"If you don't make mistakes, you aren't really trying."

-Coleman Hawkins

So, what ingredients do you need in a perfect piece of video marketing?

Well, not much marketing, for one. (But we'll get to that.)

First, let's break down some of the different forms of video marketing and see which may or may not be a good fit for your business needs.

VIDEO FORM NO. 1: TALKING-HEAD EXPERT STUFF

Just like it sounds.

This is somebody on your team, or maybe you, talking straight to a camera or smartphone mounted on a tripod, offering helpful tips or insight into a particular topic.

It's simple, powerful and staggeringly effective for building rapport with viewers.

Mostly, because so many videos of this kind are truly abysmal. (Just head over to the freakshow that is YouTube to verify.)

As with any video: audio quality is huge. Nobody will tolerate you talking 40 feet away from the camera.

It can also be a bit scary, especially for people who aren't uber-comfortable on camera; in which case a script or series of bullet points is highly recommended.

There's a reason so much of video marketing is in this form… it works.

Pros: Personable. Quick. Easy to produce. Great at building an emotional connection to you or your brand.

Cons: May require Valium for those who are frightened of being on camera.

Video Form No. 2: Screen Capture Tutorial

This is where you record what's on your computer screen, with software such as Camtasia or Screenflow, as you talk over the slide presentation.

I know. Sounds mind-numbingly boring. But it's actually great for:

☑ Product Demos

☑ Sales Videos

☑ Technical Training

☑ Big Ideas That Require Text

And you know that whole "rule" about corporate Power-Point presentations? Where you're not supposed to repeat the words on the slide?

Yeah, that doesn't apply here.

In a video, people actually like to read along as you go through the points of your presentation.

The downside is you don't get that human connection, but you know what? For some folks that's okay. If you're a bit camera-shy, this can be a great way to break into the video marketing field.

Pros: Don't even need a camera! Easy to fix glitches and mistakes. Super cheap and easy to make.

Cons: Can be boring, if not focused. Need images to make video stand out.

VIDEO FORM NO. 3: BEHIND THE SCENES

This may require you to tap into your inner Spielberg, but if you can, it's totally worth it.

Just go around your business and shoot some footage. Talk to some of your employees, give folks a look at what's it like behind the counter.

Show people that your business is…in fact…filled with people.

Even if you're a solo-preneur, people still want to see what your desk looks like, what books are on your bookshelf, what kind of bobbleheads you have in the window, etc.

We'll cover filming a bit later, but here's the absolute KEY here: get good audio.

Too many of these behind-the-scenes videos have such bad audio, that it makes them unwatchable.

And don't talk about how amazing your company is. Talk about something interesting.

Got a policy where employees can bring their dogs to work? Film it!

Have somebody on your team who can breakdance? Film it!

Is there an annual chili contest in the second floor building of your company? Film it!

This is a great way to spotlight your team, and get some cool marketing fuel in the process.

Pros: Really good (sneaky) way of marketing your brand. Fun. Boosts team morale.

Cons: Requires some editing time. Bit of technical know-how. (But not much.)

Video Form No. 4: Customer Testimonials

This is actually the most overlooked form of video marketing, but one of the most powerful.

Got a group of regular customers who love your stuff? It's imperative you put them on video.

Next time you see 'em, have them do a very brief 30-second talk about why they love your stuff.

(**Tip:** Be sure they start their response with "The reason I love (name)…" or else it will be hard to edit their response in context.)

Sell things virtually?

No problem. You can record people on Skype talking about your company, or even better…

Have them leave a voice mail message and put that into a video with a simple slideshow. (God knows why, but people just instantly believe things that are on the phone.)

Now, you want to tread carefully here. Don't make it too over-the-top. (No need to have scores of customers gush over how you are the best company that ever existed.)

But if you've got some good social proof going on, then throw in some video footage of your products or services. It can do more for your video marketing efforts than all the talking-head videos in the world.

Pros: Very effective at increasing leads. Easy to film. Virtually no work on your part.

Cons: Can get annoying quickly, if not done well. Sometimes hard to get customers to talk on-camera.

Video Form No. 5: Video Q&A

Have no idea what to do a video on?

Well, just ask people what their biggest questions/frustrations are…and then go ahead and answer them.

I had a client of mine who ran a pizza joint, and all he did was set up his iPhone and answer questions submitted to him via email.

Think his tips on helping folks create the perfect crust hurt sales?

Absolutely not! (And in a later chapter I'll show you how to track the effectiveness of your video marketing to make sure you're not wasting your time on these things.)

Video Form No. 6: Anything But…

Notice what kind of video marketing I did NOT mention?

That's right. YOU talking about how amazing/wonderful/awesome your company is.

Nobody cares. (Really.)

You can talk about virtually anything on camera, just don't go on and on about the amazing features and benefits of your latest doo-hickey. (Unless it's a sales page video, and even then…)

Not only will YouTube (the "one ring to rule them all" in terms of video distribution) probably ban your video, but it won't help you reach any of your marketing goals.

CHAPTER 1 Key Takeaways:

☑ Talking head videos are great for how-to tips and building personality into your brand.

☑ Screen capture videos are fantastic for technical training and product demos.

☑ Behind-the-scenes vids are perfect for showing a funnier/ lighter side of your biz.

☑ Testimonials from your customers are great, if done subtly.

☑ Video Q&As are a good way to help people out, and allow you to be seen as a ready-made expert.

☑ Overt marketing videos are boring and lame; and nobody wants to watch them.

Chapter 2:

Anatomy of the Perfect Video

"To express yourself needs a reason, but express-ing yourself is a reason."

-Ai Weiwei

So you got some ideas for what kind of video you might want to do.

But what do you actually put in the video?

How do you structure your video? What do you say? What do you NOT say?

And how do you make sure the video actually does something for your business, you know, besides pad your ego?

Worry not! Here's my patented (I wish) FIVE Step Video Marketing Checklist to ensure your videos stay on track and get you the results you want:

STEP NO. 1: THE BRIEF INTRO

When I say brief? I mean…brief. Not a minute. Not 30 seconds. Get in, get out.

And most importantly, tell people WHY the hell they should be watching.

This is probably the simplest step in this process, but the one most people neglect. (Watch any DIY how-to videos on YouTube and this will become abundantly clear.)

So, what should you put in your intro?

This is what I say, and I hardly ever deviate from this formula:

"Hi there, it's Michael from Punk Rock Marketing. And in this short video, I'm going to cover the No.1 reason why Facebook is a spawn of Satan intent on bringing down Western Civilization with its desire to plant electrodes in our brain…and what you can do about it."

Okay, so let's break it down a bit further:

"Hi, it's Michael…"

☑ Put your name and your company in there. Fast. You have no idea where people will watch your video, so get your branding out there right away.

"In this short video…"

☑ Tell 'em it's going to be short. This is key. Lets them know they won't be sitting in their chair for a hundred years as you show them how to change a spark plug.

"I'm going to cover…"

☑ Tell them what they will get from watching the video. What solution will your video provide? What insight will it cover? What PROBLEM will it solve?

STEP NO. 2: THE STATE OF THINGS

This is where you take a slight step back. And tell people WHY it's important they know this thing you're going to tell them.

They may already intuitively know this, but this brief section will help nail it home, and give them confidence in your ability to help them.

Again, keep this brief.

I might do something like this:

"Facebook has built its empire on user data. But how do they get that data? With tiny electrodes they plant in our brain when we're sleeping next to our smartphone. That's how!

"Here's how you can keep the electrodes from invading your body..."

Notice how it moves seamlessly into the next step, which is...

STEP NO. 3: THE MEAT AND POTATOES

This is where you instruct. Or in the case of more whimsical fare, such as the behind-the-scenes video and testimonials, fire off into the fun part.

Whatever form you're dabbling with, this is where you give up the goods. Where you deliver on the promise you set forth in the brief intro.

Here are a few tips to ensure your Meat and Potatoes don't go completely off the rails:

☑ **Don't ramble.** Just stick to the points.

☑ **Lists are great.** If you can tell us the three steps, the five techniques, the four tactics to solve the problem....people will love you for it.

☑ **Keep the number of steps reasonable**. Don't do 19 ways to lower your car insurance bills. Do seven. Or one.

☑ **Just cover one idea in your video.** You're not trying to cure cancer. You're just trying to solve one problem. (Even if that solution has three or four parts to it.)

☑ **Remember people don't know as much as you do.** If there's a lot of technical jargon or complex ideas, try to keep things simple.

☑ **Tell stories.** People love personal anecdotes. (As long as they relate to the point. If not, cut 'em.)

☑ **Don't be boring**.

Step No. 4: The Action Steps

This is where you lay out the simple step-by-step blueprint you outlined in Step No.3 into easily digestible chunks of info anybody can understand.

In my Facebook example:

"First, you cover your head in tin foil. Step two, you bury your iPhone thirty feet below ground…."

If you're doing a talking-head video, and have a bit of editing savvy, then you could throw up a quick text image of the steps at the end of the video.

But the key thing is: give people something they can take action on right now. (Even though most of them won't.)

Step No. 5: The Call to Action

Okay, you've been a super-cool awesome person. You've given them some info and helped improve their lives. (Sorta.)

Now, it's time to pay it forward. And, trust me, they will.

Obligation is absolutely hard-wired in our brain, so if somebody does us a solid we feel the need to pay it back.

So, here's what you do…in the call to action I usually ask people to do two things:

1. Share or comment on my video

2. Grab a free offer/coupon I'm offering

Here's an example:

"If you've enjoyed my anarchist ramblings about the cabal that

is Facebook be sure to Facebook like, tweet, or comment in the field below.

"And if you'd like a FREE copy of my new ebook, "7 Ways Facebook is Trying to Eat Your Soul From the Inside Out," head on over to punkrockmarketing.com to get instant access."

The cool thing about this verbiage is that even if they don't take advantage of your offer, they can still help you out by making your video more popular.

But if they do take advantage of the offer, after having watched you talk for 2.5 minutes, they are very much a qualified (if Facebook-paranoid) lead.

CHAPTER 2 KEY TAKEAWAYS:

☑ Start your video with a brief intro that tells people what they can expect to find out by watching.

☑ Follow that up with a short description of why the topic of the video is important.

☑ Get into the meat of your video. Don't ramble!

☑ Give viewers action steps they can use. Instantly!

☑ End your video with a call to action that asks people to social share and head over to your website to pre-qualify themselves.

Chapter 3:

Getting Geared Up on the Ultra Cheap

"You can fool all the people all the time...if the advertising is right and the budget is big enough."

-Joseph E. Levine

Video equipment is just like computers, makeup or Fender Telecaster guitars.

You can get as complicated and expensive, or as simple and bare-bones, as you like.

Much of it will depend on your personality.

I'm weird. I LIKE to edit video. (Maybe it's the OCD control-freak in me.)

So a good video-editing software is a MUST for me - while knowing which F-stop setting or white balance control to alter on a camera puts me in a coma.

So, when it comes to camera choice I want something that looks great out of the box...not something I have to fuss with for hours.

That said, here are my recommendations for the gear you'll need (and may want someday) as you delve into the fabulous world of video marketing.

Remember there are really only THREE MUSTS for video: good audio, something to record on, and something to say.

Everything else is just decoration.

Video Gear Must No. 1: The Microphone

What??? But what about the camera? Don't you need a good camera first?

I'm telling you, audio is your most important piece of video marketing gear.

The quality difference between the cheapest HD camcorder and the most expensive digital SLR is NOTHING compared to the quality difference between internal (built-in) microphones and external sound-capturing devices.

Ultra Cheap Option-Lavalier Microphone ($25-$100)

This is a simple tie-clip microphone (Amazon link: http://punkrockmarketing.com/lavmic) that attaches to your lapel and plugs in directly into the camera.

I can usually find one of these at Radio Shack for about $25, but there are a ton of these on Amazon, including the Sony ECM series. (If you're going to do a bunch of talking-head vids, go for a condenser lav mic. It'll be worth it in the long run.)

Tip: Run the lapel wire under your shirt to avoid making the video look super ghetto.

ELITE OPTION-WIRELESS LAVALIER MICROPHONE ($500-$700)

I don't expect you to get one of these right out the gate. But if you start making extra moolah from your video marketing efforts, then adding a wireless lavalier microphone (Amazon link: http://punkrockmarketing.com/wirelessmic) to your toolbox will be well worth it.

The sound is quite good, considering you're on a wireless channel, and it gives you a ton of flexibility in terms of movement and location. (You can even record any live presentations you give.)

Tip: Don't go for the ultra-cheap wireless units. (Models under $100.) They ain't worth it.

EXTRA ITEM - IPHONE LAV MIC ADAPTER ($25)

If you plan on shooting exclusively with your smartphone or tablet computer, then you'll need an iPhone adapter (Amazon link: http://punkrockmarketing.com/iphoneadapter) to plug in your lav mic.

Bonus: You can get a splitter that lets you get audio from two sources. Great for interviews!

VIDEO GEAR MUST-HAVE NO. 2: THE CAMERA

We're here. We're finally gonna get you a camera. (But wait! You might already have one lurking in your shirt pocket.)

Here's a breakdown of some options you have on the camera recording side:

Ultra-Cheap Option - Your SmartPhone (Free-$500)

My uncle ran a videography business in the late 80s. His equipment cost him $30,000.

Today he could do everything for under $50.

That's because the smartphone you hold in your hand, and will hold in the years to come, can produce some AMAZING quality video.

Now, if you don't have a smartphone, don't run out and go buy one just for the video capabilities. It ain't THAT good.

But if you have an Android phone or an iPhone, you've got all you need to produce amazing video. (As long as you know what you're doing; we'll go over that in more detail later.)

Semi-Cheap Option- Rugged Adventure Cameras $95-$200

If you plan on doing a lot of action video — maybe, you run a ski lodge and want to film on the slopes, or you're a surf instructor who wants to shoot some footage in the water — then there are plenty of cheap camera options, such as the GoPro or the Sony ActionCam, that will produce amazing video quality in a variety of rough settings.

The cool thing about these cameras is they're tough and can film in virtually any setting. Trouble is their sound quality often sucks. (Though they improve with each new version.)

Mix up your action shots with some microphone-assisted talking segments to get some very usable quality stuff.

Elite Option - Prosumer Camera ($500-$2500)

The more you spend, the more features you can get with

your video camera. Like better lenses, more controls, more stabilization and better ergonomics.

You wouldn't think ergonomics would make a difference. Wait till you have to hold a camera for ten minutes without shaking, and you'll see what a difference it makes.

If you do decide to spend some money on a nicer camera, I recommend you go with a Sony or Canon prosumer video camera.

There are tons of nice camcorders out there, but these two manufacturers tend to have the best lenses…which are probably the most expensive, and most important, part of a camera.

VIDEO GEAR MUST-HAVE NO. 3: TRIPOD

Unless you want your videos to induce vertigo in your viewers, you're going to need a tripod. Here are a few options:

SMARTPHONE TRIPODS - ($5-$50)

These can range from the arm tripods (Amazon link: http://punkrockmarketing.com/phonearmtripod), ones in which you wrap them around nearly any surface, or traditional stand-on-the-floor models (Amazon link: http://punkrockmarketing.com/phonelegtripod).

Popular brands include Gorilla and Joby, but whatever floats your boat should work.

CAMCORDER OPTION - ($19-$50)

This will depend mostly on your filming needs. If you're just going to shoot inside, go with one of the cheap, light tripods (http://punkrockmarketing.com/tripod). Nothing more than $25.

If you're going to shoot outside a lot, particularly in windy conditions, you might need something a little more durable, but heavy. (You might even need a few sandbags to hold down the camera.)

Either way, I find tripods generally have the shelf life of a reality TV show. (About eight months.)

A FEW THOUGHTS ON LIGHTING

Please, don't go out spending a ton of money on lighting unless you're a big video dork like me. (It's really not necessary, unless you're filming in a cave.)

The best lighting is always the sun. (So try to shoot outside if you can.)

If you do find your usual go-to film spot is a bit on the dark side, it is nice to have some portable lighting to throw in there.

Buy a couple of cheap clip-on desk lights. These will allow you to put lighting almost anywhere and give your videos some much needed warmth.

CHAPTER 3 KEY TAKEAWAYS:

☑ Audio is super important. Invest in a lavalier microphone of some kind to improve your video quality.

☑ Your smartphone is a fantastic HD camera. (As long as you've got external audio.)

☑ Tripods are flimsy, but required. (You may even need a sandbag or two.)

☑ Buy some cheap desk lamps for a quick infusion of light into your video settings.

Chapter 4:

Your Super- Quick 5-Minute Film School

"If you can't explain it to a six-year-old, you don't understand it yourself."

-Albert Einstein

Ya don't have to be Fellini to make great video marketing content.

But there are a few, simple rules to making any type of filmed media…

And knowing these rules can make you look way more talented and professional than you actually are.

So, here is my super brief Five-Minute Film School Tutorial that you can use to ensure your videos are watchable, compelling and that they communicate your message in the best way possible.

FILM-SCHOOL TIP NO. 1: KEEP THE CAMERA STILL

I know there's a zoom button on your camera. That doesn't mean you should use it.

The problem with the zoom function on most camcorders, and especially smartphones, is that they make the lens infinitely more sensitive to things like light, contrast…and to your constant moving back and forth.

And, believe me, you're moving even if you're "just" holding the camera still.

So, put your video device on a tripod whenever you can. And if you do need to go "handheld," use a nearby wall or chair to brace yourself.

And if you do "move in" to shoot something close, physically move the camera in. (Not the zoom.) It'll look much better in the long run.

FILM-SCHOOL TIP NO. 2: KEEP THE LIGHT BEHIND YOU

Most photographers know this trick pretty well, but if you're new to any kind of camera operation it's a good rule to keep the sun, or major light source, behind you as you film.

The reason is instantly clear to anybody who's filmed on a sunny day. (Direct sunlight makes the subject's face dark and under-exposed.)

Also, if you're filming outside, it's good to know that early morning and late afternoon are the best times to film.

Noontime is the absolute worst. (Mid-day sun tends to make everybody look like zombies. And nobody likes to look like a zombie. Even zombies.)

FILM-SCHOOL TIP NO. 3: KEEP THE CENTRAL SUBJECT OUT OF THE MIDDLE

This one actually surprises some people. I mean, aren't you supposed to put the video subject in the middle of the frame?

Actually, no. It looks sorta weird…and way too geometric.

Instead, put the subject off to the side, with an interesting background filling in the rest of the shot. This will make the video look dynamic and interesting. (Even if the person talking isn't.)

FILM-SCHOOL TIP No. 4: DON'T LEAVE TOO MUCH HEADROOM

Headroom is that space between a person's head and the top of the frame. It's okay to have a little bit, you don't want to cut someone's head off at the forehead.

But you don't want to have too much room at the top either. There's an old photography trick, called the Rule of Thirds, which works great here.

Simply divide the frame into three equidistant horizontal lines (like the flag of Germany) and make sure the person's head is somewhere near the top half of the frame.

FILM-SCHOOL TIP No. 5: ON-CAMERA ETIQUETTE

When it comes to being on-camera, here are a few guidelines to maximize your appearance and embrace your inner Anderson Cooper:

- ☑ Don't wear sunglasses. People WANT to see your eyes.
- ☑ Wear mid-range colors. (Blue, green, black.) No stripes and no white. (Takes attention away from the eyes.)
- ☑ No hats. (Distracts from the face.)
- ☑ Don't read from a script. Your eyes will look shifty, and unless you're Katie Couric it'll be tough to pull off.

Film-School Tip No. 6: Focus on Helping (Not Your Performance)

If you try to "perform" on camera, if you think you have to somehow conjure the vibe of your local TV news anchor in order to do well on video, you are mistaken.

The opposite is true.

The camera has an amazing ability to capture who you are. (Even if you don't want it to.)

And if your entire mindset is all about:

"Look at me! I'm on camera. I'm an expert! Buy my stuff! While supplies last!"

It won't work. (Or not as well as it could.) But if you step into the frame and think...

"There's problem a lot of people have. Here's how I figured out how to solve it. Hope it works for you. Talk to you soon..."

You. Will. Crush. It.

Because so much of the crap videos out there are people yelling at the camera, hoping those "thousands" of viewers will take action NOW!

But if you, or your team, get on camera, and just help solve people's problems, there's no way the competition - what little of it there will be - can stop you.

CHAPTER 4 KEY TAKEAWAYS:

- ☑ Keep the camera still. Seriously.
- ☑ Always keep the sun to your back. (Morning and afternoon are good times to shoot.)
- ☑ Put the subject off to the side to mix things up.
- ☑ Keep the subject's head in the top third of the frame.
- ☑ Don't wear sunglasses, white shirts or hats. Stick to mid-range colors like blue or green.
- ☑ Focus on solving people's problems to get past on-camera nervousness.

Chapter 5:

Crashing the YouTube Party

"Hobbies of any kind are boring, except for people who have the same hobby."

-Dave Barry

When it comes to looking for a place to house your video marketing efforts, there really is YouTube…and everybody else.

YouTube isn't just simply the largest video-sharing site in the world.

It's the second-largest search engine in the world.

Read that again.

The second-largest SEARCH ENGINE.

That means, when it comes to Internet traffic, there's Google, then YouTube, then Amazon, then Facebook…

…and then way, way, way down the list are other video-sharing sites such as Vimeo and Viddler and Voohoo (or whatever the hell else they're called.)

This doesn't mean that things won't ever change, or that you shouldn't place your videos on the other sites. (In a later chapter, I'll show you a super-easy quick way to do so.)

It's just that, when I outline my video-marketing strategy for a project, I generally spend 99.7% of my time worrying about YouTube. (And then, in between episodes of "Law and Order," I think about the other sites.)

YouTube has the eyeballs. (And by last count, nearly 1 billion unique visitors a month.) So that's where your videos need to go.

So, here is my SIX STEP process to uploading your video to YouTube that will boost your exposure and help you add a bunch of new leads into your marketing funnel of awesomeness:

STEP No.1: CHOOSE A KEYWORD FOR THE NAME OF YOUR VIDEO

In case you've been living under a Wi-Fi disabled rock, keywords are the semantic phrases people use to find stuff on the Internet.

And since Google OWNS YouTube it would behoove us to figure out how people are searching for stuff, so our video can show up, not just on YouTube, but in Google as well.

Here's how you do it:

1. Head over to the Google Keyword Planner tool. (Just search for the phrase "Google Keyword planner" and you'll find it.)
2. Click on "Search for new keyword and ad group ideas"
3. Enter a couple of keywords related to your video topics.
4. Hit "Get Ideas."
5. Click on the "Keyword Ideas" tab.
6. Hit "search" again.
7. Start browsing the "keyword ideas" below to find keyword phrases that have AT LEAST 1000 "Local Searches a Month" (Don't worry about the "competition." You won't have any.)
8. Find a keyword that matches your video, and fit it into your video title somehow.

Say I'm doing a video on "bathroom renovation." Well, I might have just assumed the best thing would be to title my video "How to Renovate Your Bathroom."

But in looking at the good old keyword tool I see that the phrase "bathroom remodeling" gets a TON more searches. (8100, in fact! That's a lot!)

So instead I might want to title my video something like:

☑ Bathroom Remodeling 101

☑ Bathroom Remodeling Do's and Dont's

☑ Bathroom Remodeling Tips

☑ Bathroom Remodeling Made Easy

You get the idea. What you don't want to do is put the keyword phrase at the end of the title, such as: "Your Ultimate and Amazing Guide to All Things Bathroom Remodeling."

Get the good stuff (and keywords) in at the beginning.

STEP NO.2: RENAME YOUR VIDEO FILE WITH A KEYWORD

This one's a trick not many people know about. But the name of your video file directly relates to its ranking and relevancy in YouTube. (And thereby its ranking in good old Google.)

And what do you name it?

The keyword you want to rank for, of course.

So using the example above, you'd name your file "Bathroom_Remodeling_101" NOT "Video_1."

Now this is something you have to change before you upload it to YouTube. But it's super easy.

Just click on the video file name until it's highlighted, type in the keyword…and you're done.

Step No. 3: Make your youtube channel

NICHE-FOCUSED

If you haven't already created a YouTube account, then this won't be a problem.

But if you've got a channel and it's got videos of your kids playing soccer, excerpts of you singing bad 80s karaoke and that awesome slideshow of your trip to Yosemite…

…then I highly, highly recommend you create a new, separate YouTube channel (you'll need a separate Gmail account as well) that just focuses on your video marketing.

I know it seems like a pain, but it's also another part of Google's determination of the relevancy of videos.

If all your videos are about "lawn care," then it will assume your YouTube channel is about "lawn care." If your video library is a hodge-podge or random pixelated crap, then you won't get that same "benefit of the doubt."

And if you're not sure what to name your YouTube channel, just pick one of the keywords off the research you just did. (Instead of Joe's Pizza Joint…you could do Best Denver Pizza and take advantage of the extra Google juice.)

Step No. 4: Write a Killer Description for Your Video

So, here's where most people royally screw up. They either have crappy descriptions or no description at all.

Which is quite sad, because the description of your YouTube video is primo real estate. (And super important to how your video will rank in the good old search engines.)

So, your description needs to have four parts and it must be in this order:

1. **A hyperlink to your website.** This must be first and it must include the http://....etc... Example: http://punk-rockmarketing.com

2. **Reiterate the FREE/awesome offer you made in the video.** "Head over to punkrockmarketing.com for your FREE copy of my Facebook Brain Protector eBook."

3. **Describe your video.** You are given 1,000 characters here. Use as much of that as you can. And be sure to include that handy-dandy keyword you found earlier a few times in there.

4. **Give out your digits.** If ya got a Facebook page, Twitter account, Pinterest doo-dad...whatever...put it here. (Remember to include the http:// part.)

5. **Repeat the FREE offer + your hyperlink.** Example: "Don't forget to head over to http://punkrockmarketing. com for your FREE copy of my Facebook brain protector eBook."

STEP NO. 5: BEG, BORROW AND STEAL TAGS

This one is a super-sneaky ninja trick. But it's a super-sneaky ninja trick that totally works.

One of the key factors in ranking your video is the tags you use when uploading your video, and the relationship those tags have to the other top related videos in your area of expertise.

For instance: If I wanted to upload a video around the keyword "Denver car insurance" then I would want to find out what video was ranking number one for that keyword.

You find this out by doing a simple search in YouTube under that phrase and find out who comes out at the top.

Once I find out who was on top, I would literally want to

copy all of their tags and put them into the tag field of my video. (And maybe add a couple of extra tags of my own.)

And once upon a time this was super easy.

But then people (like me) were gaming the system. So YouTube decided to "hide" the tags.

But just because they're hidden doesn't mean you can't find them.

All you gotta do is:

☑ Click on the #1 YouTube video for the phrase you want to rank for.

☑ While the video is playing, right-click on your mouse and choose "View Page Source."

☑ You'll see a bunch of gibberish-looking code. (Don't freak out.) Hit Control-F on your keyboard and put in "keywords."

☑ This will highlight the area of the code related to keywords.

☑ You will see an area that says something like: "<meta name="keywords" content="Denver Pizza joint">

☑ Grab everything in the "Denver Pizza joint" space after the "content="

☑ Delight in the fact that you have out-smarted YouTube… and the world!

Step No. 6: Upload Your Video

Here's the easy part.

You just click on "upload" at the top of the YouTube navigation and upload your video file, enter your title, description and tags…and you are ready to begin your YouTube world domination.

CHAPTER 5 KEY TAKEAWAYS:

☑ Choose a video title that leverages a keyword that gets at least 1,000 searches a month.

☑ Re-title the file name of your video using your desired keyword.

☑ Keep your YouTube channel focused only on video marketing — no personal vids.

☑ Include a "http://" hyperlink in the beginning of your description.

☑ Use all 1000 characters of the description if you can.

☑ "Borrow" tags from other high-performing videos using the "view page source" trick.

Chapter 6:

How to Promote the Hell Out of Your Video

"I am always doing that which I cannot do, in order that I may learn how to do it."

-Pablo Picasso

If you've gone to the trouble of making a series of videos, then you damn well want to get them in front of the largest number of eyeballs possible.

But most people throw up a video or two on YouTube and simply "wait" for the masses to come banging down their door to give them money.

Sorry, but it don't work that way.

YouTube requires a bit of hustle and some promotional savvy to work. But the cool thing is, once you've got a system (which I'll share with you here) and work that system consistently, it becomes really easy to out-pace the competition in no time.

"GENTLEMEN, YOU CAN'T FIGHT IN HERE. THIS IS THE WAR ROOM."

There are basically two different areas of promoting your videos:

1. Stuff you can do INSIDE YouTube.

2. Stuff you can do OUTSIDE YouTube.

Let's start with the OUTSIDE stuff. It's super easy, and doesn't require much brain power.

Strategy No. 1: Promote the Video Everywhere!

Once you upload your video and it's done "cooking" in the YouTube kitchen, you will get a unique URL. (Example: http://youtube.com/watch=S1uDnIP9L)

With that web address in tow, you can now promote that video on social networks like Facebook, LinkedIn, Twitter, Pinterest, Tumblr, your email newsletter, etc.

The key thing is to ASK people to "like" it or "share" it when they watch the video. Lots of social activity around your video, especially when it's first uploaded, is a big sign to Google that this video is "important" and should be given prominent place in the search engines.

Strategy No. 2: Build Some Links to Your Video

Okay, this technique is a bit on the shady side. (And by shady, I mean if you tried doing this with your own website, Google would give it a cold, hard slap.)

But it totally frickin' works.

What you're going to do is build backlinks to the video page.

In the crazy, strange world of SEO (Search Engine Optimization), most people spend time and money trying to get their own websites ranked super quick. (Which doesn't work very often.)

But for a big "authority" site, like YouTube, it can work exceedingly well.

So, here's what you do:

☑ Head over to Fiverr.com (http://fiverr.com). This is a site where people offer services of all kinds — some awesome, some just plain weird — for five dollars.

☑ Buy THREE "gigs" for a whopping fifteen dollars. Search for "SEO" services. And choose people with high ratings.

☑ Have the gig master build backlinks to your video around your primary keyword.

STRATEGY NO. 3: STOP THE PRESSES

If you have a little extra money to spend (about $25) and you've optimized your video to this point, then it's definitely worth your while to send out a press release touting your video.

Huh?

A press release? About a YouTube video?

Before you freak out and tell me that your video isn't newsworthy and nobody would read a press release about it…

First off, you should see some of the crap people send press releases on. (It's hysterical.)

Secondly, we are not sending it out in the hope that Brian Williams of NBC News is going to ask us to join the broadcast.

We are doing it for the Google backlink love. And Google REALLY respects press releases. (God knows why, most of them are pretty awful.)

For $25 you can head over to a site like WebWire (http://webwire.com) and shoot out a press release about your video.

A couple of keys:

- ☑ Write a decent headline by focusing on the problem you're solving. Example: Chicago Pizza King Reveals the Secret to Homemade Crust."

- ☑ Write it in third person. As if you were having an interview with yourself.

- ☑ Make sure you include links back to the video, along with the keywords we researched earlier.

Trust me, do these three things and you will be light-years ahead of the rest of the schmucks who put their crap on YouTube.

"FORGET IT, JAKE. IT'S CHINATOWN."

Okay, now let's jump into the strange morass of insanity and awesomeness that is promotion inside the YouTube universe.

The three main goals of your videos on planet YouTube are "likes," "shares," and "subscribers."

The higher these numbers, the more the Google/YouTube empire will see your video as an authority and you will blow your (feeble) competition out of the water.

So, how do we get more of all that YouTube community goodness?

Here are my FOUR strategies for getting more people into your YouTube army:

Strategy No. 1: Create Annotations

Annotations are a way to create linkable text overlays onto your video. (You've probably seen these in the annoying "text commentary" that people put on their videos.)

But you can use them to:

☑ Encourage people to subscribe to your YouTube channel.

☑ Provide links to your other videos.

☑ Link over to other YouTube users' videos who offer more resources.

Annotations are super easy to create. All you do is:

☑ Click on the annotations button below your video.

☑ Let the video play to the point where you want the annotation.

☑ Add the annotation!

Strategy No. 2: Create Keyword-Friendly Playlists

Here's another technique a lot of YouTube creators miss out on. (And it's so frickin' easy.)

All you do is create a playlist around a specific keyword that includes your videos and a mix of other people's videos.

The key thing here is to include other people's stuff, not just your own. However, avoid adding your competitor's videos, unless you would like to help their business out.

Strategy No. 3: Respond to Comments Within 24 Hours

I have to admit, I'm not as good about this as I should be. But one of the biggest factors in determining the "authority" of your YouTube channel is your engagement with people who leave comments.

Especially within a day or so of the comment being left.

So, try to check in every couple of days to respond to comments. (You should get an email each time a comment is left.)

But…PLEASE…do not engage with negative commenters. (It's not worth it. Trust me.)

STRATEGY No.4: BUILD YOUR SUBSCRIBER BASE FAST!

The best thing about subscribers is they comment. (Sometimes too much.)

And even more importantly, subscribers get an email from YouTube every time you upload a new video. This ensures all your future videos will have plenty of social buzz around them.

So, what's the catch?

Well, doing this is a bit of a manual process. (In the next chapter, I'll show you a tool that can automate it.)

One of the most effective ways I've found to boost the views of my YouTube videos, literally overnight, is to "send messages" to my target audience inviting them to: **Check out my new video and/or subscribe to my channel.**

Say I run an e-commerce site that specializes in Minor League Baseball apparel. (An interesting market, by the way.)

Well, instead of spending tons of money on Google PPC traffic, I could create a video on the Top 5 Coolest Baseball Caps in Minor League Baseball.

And then I could find out who the fans of those teams are, by searching for videos relating to those teams. (And sending messages to people who've commented on those videos.)

It's quite an easy process, you just:

☑ Search for videos related to your subject.

☑ Locate people who've commented recently — within the last two months.

☑ Click on their name to bring up their profile page.

☑ Click on the "send message" button. (Located in the drop-down arrow on the right side, under their name.)

☑ Send them a message along the lines of: "Hey. I noticed you're a fan of the Sacramento Bear Cats. I just made a video of the Top 5 Baseball caps in Minor League baseball and they made the cut. Thought you'd want to check it out. Thanks!"

Now, I know that sounds quite manual. (It is.)

I'll show you a tool in the next chapter that can handle it super easily, but in the interim maybe you could get an intern or some aimless teenager (maybe one who shares your last name) to do it for you.

No joke, this is one technique that will put your face in front hundreds of new people each day, and if you follow it up with the rest of the techniques in this chapter you'll be dominating the YouTube universe in no time.

CHAPTER 6 KEY TAKEAWAYS:

☑ Promote your YouTube video by sharing your unique URL on your various social media properties.

☑ Buy a few SEO gigs over at Fiverr.com to build some keyword-focused backlinks to your video.

☑ Write and distribute a press release about your video. (Nobody does this.)

☑ Create annotations for your videos that have clear calls-to-action AND links to your external site.

☑ Build some keyword-friendly YouTube playlists for extra exposure.

☑ Try to respond to all comments to your video within a day or two. (Skip the negative ones.)

☑ Send messages to commenters of similar videos inviting them to subscribe to your channel.

Chapter 7:

Super Advanced Ninja YouTube Tactics

"Great thoughts speak to the thoughtful mind, but great actions speak to all mankind."

-Emily P. Bissell

Before we jump into the deep part of the video marketing tool, let me just say...

...if you follow the tips I've outlined so far, and there's not a ton of competition out there for you in the YouTube stratosphere, then everything we've gone over to this point should be sufficient.

If you're a local business, chances are the restaurant or business down the street is not going to be employing the same strategies. And you're likely to crush them on the video side in a matter of weeks.

But if you're in a more-competitive market, say something in the weight-loss or financial-services markets, then you're going to find there are a lot more water buffaloes at the trough.

So, below are my THREE Super-Advanced YouTube Marketing Tactics you can use to totally destroy the competition and reign supreme as the YouTube King of your market:

Warning: These tactics are a bit technical and dorky. Consult your local teenage hacker if the methods detailed aren't clear.

Ninja Tactic No. 1: Feed the RSS Monster

I'll be honest, I don't really understand how RSS works. I mean I know what it is. RSS stands for (Really Simple Syndication), and refers to a technology that helps organize and distribute content around the Internet. (RSS Feed readers such as Google Reader and Feedly use them.)

And I also know it is dying as a mode of consuming media. (You can thank Facebook for that.)

But I don't care about any of that. All I care about is how feeds build super-quick bridges to my content. (Namely, my YouTube videos.)

And, quite simply, it works as a quick-and-dirty promotional tool to create little freeways around the Internet that lead straight to my videos.

Now because each of your YouTube videos are static web locations, not a constantly changing feed, you have to do a bit of manual work to make this strategy happen. (But it's really, really easy.)

Here's what you do:

1. **Grab the URL** of your YouTube video.

2. **Head over to Html2Rss.com**. This site allows you to create a feed from any web URL.

3. **Submit your video URL** and create a feed.

4. **Copy the feed URL** Html2Rss gives you.

5. **Head over to Ping-O-Matic** (http://pingomatic.com) and Pingler (http://pingler.com). These are pinging sites that let the world know your RSS feed exists.

6. **Enter your new feed URL** in the fields provided, along with your keyword, and ping the feed. (You only have to do this once. Not continually.)

Ninja Tactic No. 2: External Annotations

So, you remember those annotations I talked about in the last chapter?

Well, for years that was the only kind of annotation you could place in your video. The big limitation was that you couldn't link out to your external website.

But, recently, YouTube started allowing creators to add external annotations that allow you to send people to your website.

I repeat: viewers can click on your video and head straight over to your website. (Super cool!)

So here's how you do it:

1. **Go to your YouTube channel settings.** Can be found under youtube.com/dashboard.

2. **Activate monetization.** Click on monetization and follow the steps laid out by YouTube.

3. **Add your website.** Click on associated website under Channel Settings. This will ensure you're not a total spammer, which I hope you aren't.

4. **Go back to the video you want to add the annotation to.**

5. **Click "annotations."** (Just like before.)

6. When you **add the annotation** in your video check the "link" box.

7. **Add your website in the field provided.**

8. **Save changes!**

It's way easier than it sounds. And considering how utterly lazy people really are, it can be a great way to drive more traffic back to your website.

Ninja Tactic No. 3: Your Very Own YouTube Toolbox

Back in the last chapter I talked about how sending private messages to viewers who are in your ideal target audience was the BEST, FASTEST way to build up your subscriber base…

…and get tons and tons of new people in your good old marketing funnel FAST!

My only lament was that, due to YouTube's rather strict messaging policies, it was a bit time-consuming to manually send out these messages.

Well, there is a tool that can automate it for you.

It's called Tube Toolbox. (You can download a FREE TRIAL of the software at PunkRockMarketing.com/Toolbox.)

And, I'm not exaggerating when I say that implementing this tool was like giving my video efforts marketing amphetamines. (Without all the hair loss and rambling conversations with the TV.)

I won't get into the super nitty-gritty details of how it works, they're a bit technical, but in a nutshell, here's what it does:

1. **You find a video with a bunch of commenters** who you'd like to message. (Your ideal customers.)

2. **You create a message template** of what you'd like to say to these commenters. (Example: "Hey There! Check out my new vid on Facebook Satanism!")

3. **Tube Toolbox scrapes the video** to find the user profile info for all those commenters.

4. **Tube Toolbox SLOWLY sends out those messages**, six at a time, to all of those commenters. (Thereby following YouTube's terms of service.)

Now, the downside is this can take quite awhile, especially if you're trying to message hundreds, if not thousands, of people.

But I've gotten absolutely amazing results from it. (And reached a bunch of people I never would have without it.)

Tip: If you do pick up a copy of Tube Toolbox, try to throw it onto an older (ish) laptop or desktop that you don't use all the time.

I haven't asked you to buy any fancy tools up to this point, and you don't have to have Tube Toolbox in order to have YouTube success, but I unreservedly recommend the tool. (The guys are great, the support is awesome, and the forum is friendly and helpful.)

CHAPTER 7 KEY TAKEAWAYS:

- ☑ Create an RSS Feed of your video and promote by pinging, for added promotional boost.

- ☑ Use external annotations to make it easier for viewers to check out your other web properties.

- ☑ The author highly, highly recommends Tube Toolbox for building your subscriber base up, and exponentially increasing your overall video views.

Epilogue:
Conquering the World One Video at a Time

In a previous life I wanted to work in radio. (I guess something about living just above the poverty line appealed to me.)

Anyway, for a brief time I actually got to work as an intern for a local sports talk radio station. (You know, the kind where two mentally-imbalanced individuals argue about whether the designated hitter is responsible for the downfall of Western civilization.)

I remember late one night I was messing around in the studio, working on my "reel." (This is a demo that would-be on-air talent sends around in the hopes of getting a gig.)

I was doing my melodramatic intro — "Hey all you sports fans out there! It's Crazy Mike! And I want to hear from YOU!" — when the grizzled, old station director walked by.

He popped his head in and gave me one of the best marketing lessons I've ever learned.

He said, as radio professionals we "experience" the audience as a large group of people. But an audience does not "experience" radio as a member of an audience.

They experience radio as a one-to-one conversation. (One in which they happen to not have access to a microphone.)

And when you say something like "Hey sports fans!" it destroys the intimate connection an audience has with you. And people don't quite feel as emotional about the things you're talking about, nor are they likely to stick around, while you break away to air some car dealership commercials.

And you end up reaching nobody at all.

But if you talk as ONE person talking to another PERSON, then you'll reach EVERYBODY.

"Is This Real Life?"

This YouTube stuff is addicting.

You'll create a series of videos and in a month or so you'll have 2,000 views, 100 comments and tons of new leads and you'll think I just need to scale this.

I need to make more videos, and get more subscribers, and get more likes, and hire more video people, and buy some latest YouTube Hack automation tool that can do it all in five minutes or less.

Just remember, video works best when the person on camera is having a conversation with one person.

Trying to solve one person's problems. (Maybe even their own.)

People will email you and write to you to say they felt like you were talking just to "them."

Which you were.

If you can stick with that philosophy and not worry about what you look like on camera, or what aspect ratio your video should be, and do at least a couple videos a month…then there is absolutely nothing the competition can do to stop you from reaching even your most ambitious business goals. (Short of implanting Facebook electrodes into your brain.)

*   *   *

Vexed by Video? Worry not, young Jedi.

To grab your very own FREE Video Marketing Cheat Sheet, head over to **PunkRockMarketing.com** TODAY and get instant access to your very own Video Marketing Checklist.

It's so easy, a Kardashian can do it! (With a little help from Bruce Jenner.)

Again, head over to PunkRockMarketing.com TODAY and get your FREE Video Marketing Cheat Sheet.

And if you have any questions, just drop me a line at Michael@punkrockmarketing.com.

Okay...it's time for the MOST popular social network on the planet. That's right you're ready for...

Vol.3
of the Punk Rock
Marketing
COLLECTION

FACEBOOK MARKETING

THAT DOESN'T SUCK

Michael Clarke

Prologue:
Yeah, But How Do You
Make Money With Facebook

I hate Facebook.

I hate "engaging" with annoying friends from high school who share every photo of their zip-lining vacation in Costa Rica. (Especially when I'm sitting at a desk, working.)

I hate "connecting" with my cousin's weekly political rant on what's wrong with Washington politics and how as a pool cleaner he has all the answers to fix it.

I don't what "being authentic" means on a media platform that barrages me with "Bubble Safari" requests and "Mafia Wars" clues and "You Should Like This Crappy Page Because Your Friends Liked This Crappy Page" suggestions.

Facebook is annoying, shallow, pretentious, invasive and... possibly criminal.

And that's why it really pains me to say this...

...when it comes to reaching the largest, most targeted customer base ANYWHERE, at the cheapest, lowest cost ANYWHERE...

...nothing works quite like Facebook.

"ALWAYS BE SELLING"

If you're reading this right now chances are you fall into one of two categories:

1. **You've tried Facebook in the past**, had lousy results, wasted a bunch of time and money and don't know what the fuss is all about. *But other people seem to be doing well with Facebook marketing and you want to know their secret.*

2. **You've avoided Facebook like the plague**. You think it's a technological fad that creates a lot of marketplace noise but doesn't actually lead to sustainable profits. *But other people seem to be doing well with Facebook and you want to know their secret.*

Either way, you've come to the right place.

There's no better evangelist than the converted, and I have definitely swung from hating (nearly) everything about a company who turned "friend" into a verb and designed their entire color scheme around the fact that their CEO is color blind…

…to understanding that Facebook is poised to become THE portal that people use to do everything.

Not just A portal. THE portal.

Facebook is going after every part of your experience as human being. (How you search on the Internet, buy products, read books, watch movies, find restaurants, communicate with every single person you know, etc.)

And if they accomplish just 10% of what they want to, they will be an overbearing, intrusive, obnoxious presence in our lives for decades to come.

And one that we as marketers can use to make a crapload of money.

THE MAGIC FORMULA

So, in my opinion, the big dilemma about Facebook marketing comes down to this: how do all of those "likes" and "friends" and "pages" and "posts" lead to people becoming customers?

The process is simple. It goes a little something like this:

1. Build a Facebook Page that doesn't suck
2. Fill it with fun questions and cool conversation starters
3. Attract a ton of people to like and follow your pages and posts
4. Run cheap Facebook ads to drive people to check out your products, services, contests, sweepstakes, and offers
5. Make money (and push brand-new customers into your funnel)
6. Rinse and Repeat

And that's what I'm going to show you in this book. Step by step.

I've replicated this system in a bunch of different markets, with a bunch of different buying patterns. And the only time I haven't had success is when I've deviated from this system. (Or skipped a step because I was feeling lazy.)

So if you don't mind, we're gonna leave the talk about "connecting" and "being authentic" for the other guys (and girls).

We're just going to talk about what works. (And kick some serious Facebook marketing ass in the process.)

You ready?

Chapter 1:

How to Create a Fan Page That Doesn't Suck

"When all the details fit in perfectly, something is probably wrong with the story."

-Charles Baxter

The road to hell is paved with crappy Facebook Fan Pages.

That's because creating a Facebook Fan Page is easy. (Just head over to Facebook.com/Pages and "Create a page".)

But creating a Facebook page that humans actually find, that actually shows up in both the Facebook search graph and the Google search engine results, and that actually brings in qualified leads for (nearly) FREE, requires more than just slapping your company name on a Fan Page.

It requires you to optimize key areas of your fan page.

And to do that we need to delve a bit into the chaotic and murky world of keywords.

"DON'T THINK WE'RE IN KANSAS ANYMORE"

Keywords, in case you've been living in cryogenic freeze for the past ten years, are the semantic phrases that web users type when they're looking for stuff they want, or searching for information to help them solve a problem. (Or, in the case of my nephew, the phrases he types when looking for stupid wrestling videos.)

The best and most well-known tool for finding out what these exact keywords are is the Google Keyword Tool. (It's FREE.)

The reason using a keyword analysis tool is so important is that not all keywords are created equal. You might think, and rightly so, that the following phrases would be roughly the same:

[Solutions for Hair Loss]

[Hair Loss Solutions]

Not so. The second one is the clear winner. It gets nearly 1,500 searches more a month. "Ranking" higher in the search engines for the right terms can directly affect how many new visitors/customers you get to your various web properties. (And how much moolah you can ultimately make.)

HOW TO MAKE YOUR BUSINESS GOOGLE-PROOF

So, what's this all got to do with Facebook?

Well, for years, spammers and shady Internet hucksters tried to game the search engines by stuffing their sites with keywords and creating worthless backlinks. (Backlinks are how external sites "link" back to other web properties.)

Spammers used them to boost the rankings of their website. (And increase the likelihood that their site would show up on the first page of Google.)

And, for a while, it worked.

Then one day, not so long ago, Google brought the hammer down on the whole keyword thing...and the entire Internet landscape changed.

And many (relatively) smaller websites suffered. (Mine included.)

Which only helped huge platforms like Facebook, Amazon, and Apple…as if they needed help.

Because all those keyword and backlink strategies that don't work for your website anymore, still work surprisingly well for established entities like your Facebook Fan Page.

And the cool part is, hardly anybody does this. (Or even knows that it's a strategy.)

So before we dig into what your Fan page cover photo looks like, and how you can get all those annoying "likes" that make the Facebook universe run…

…let's create your Fan Page, or tweak your existing one, and make sure it's visible and performing its absolute marketing best with these THREE Fan Page SEO Hacks:

Fan-Page SEO Hack No. 1: Put a Keyword in Your Facebook Page Name (and Username)

Fan Page Name Vs. Fan Page Username. This one always confuses people. (And no wonder, they sound exactly the same. Thanks, Facebook!)

Your Fan Page Name is the display name that shows up next to your profile thumbnail on your Fan Page. (Below the Page Name is the number of likes and number of people talking about your page.)

Your Facebook Username, on the other hand, is what is in the actual URL of your page: http://Facebook.com/MyUsername.

Both are important. And both have a huge IMPACT on your Page's SEO rankings.

Now, you don't want to go crazy with the whole keyword thing.

You don't want to do something like this for your Page Name: "*Joe's Pizza – Best Denver Pizza, Best Denver Italian, Best Calzone Denver*." Facebook will crack down on you and Facebook users will think you're a spammy jerk. (Which may or may not be true.)

That being said here's what to keep in mind regarding *Page Names*:

- ☑ **You have quite a bit of space with your Page Name.** Use it! Most marketers just throw in their business name and figure they're done, but there's a lot of space there. It's prime real estate, so use it.

- ☑ **The closer to the beginning of the page name, the more weight that page name's SEO will have.** So "San Diego Videography - Vizboo" would be better than "Vizboo - Your Ultimate Source for San Diego Videography."

- ☑ **You can create as many Facebook Pages as you want.** If your business caters to different audiences, you may want to create separate Fan pages for these segments, and take advantage of the SEO boost some keyword-laced page names can offer. (I worked with a bankruptcy attorney who created a separate Facebook page for each form of bankruptcy.)

- ☑ **Don't be too generic with your page name.** Example: "Pizza, Brews, Sports" just ain't gonna cut it. Ya gotta be specific and focused on YOUR business.

- ☑ **You can only change your page name if you've got fewer than 200 likes.** So, choose carefully and get this whole Page Name nailed down before you get too popular. Trust me, by following the tips in this book, you'll get to 200 likes in no time, so neglect this tip at your own peril.

When it comes to your *Facebook username*, you don't quite have the character space to go keyword crazy. But here are a few items of note:

☑ **Beg, borrow, and steal your way to 25 likes for your Page.** Until you got your 25 likes, you'll have to stick with an abysmal username like Facebook.com/profile.php?id=52984566. So get those 25 likes as soon as you can.

☑ **Choosing a Facebook username is like having children.** Once you have 'em, you have 'em for life. So choose wisely.

☑ **Choose something you're comfortable with.** I find with many of my properties, my Fan Page ranks well ahead of my actual website in the search-engine results. So, it's good to go with something you actually like the sound of. (And something that looks good on a business card.)

☑ **Come up with a username that's short and describes clearly what your business is about.** What's your service, benefit or product? (If you don't know, then you have bigger business issues than this book can fix.)

☑ **If somebody grabbed your username, and it does happen, choose something else related to your business.** Facebook doesn't check to see if usernames match the Facebook fan pages. They don't care. They are Facebook. So if somebody grabbed "PlumbingPatrol" and that was the actual name of my business, then I might go local, such as "SanDiegoPlumbers" or "PlumbersSanDiego" or even do something more broad such as "BestPlumberSanDiego" or "FindAPlumber."

FAN-PAGE SEO HACK NO. 2: PUT YOUR KEYWORDS (ALMOST) EVERYWHERE

So we've talked about some of the SEO benefits that a few well-placed keywords in your username and Fan Page name can do for you.

But here's where the real SEO magic happens. Lucky for us, it's an area where most marketers fail to take advantage of…the "informational" fields that are all over your Facebook Fan Page.

This would include:

- ☑ The "about" section
- ☑ The "description"
- ☑ The "short description"
- ☑ The "company overview"
- ☑ The "mission"
- ☑ The "products" field

To update these fields on your Fan page, simply click "edit page" and then select the "basic information" tab.

Now, you don't want to go overboard. You don't want to say: "*Drain Patrol is a Modesto plumber you can trust. When it comes to choosing a Modesto plumber, Drain Patrol should be your first call. We have many Modesto plumbers at your service.*"

Sounds like somebody drank a bottle of Nyquil before writing that.

But you do want to sprinkle keywords that your customers might use to "find" you. "We specialize in **data recovery**," "Jimmy Cobra voted #1 **LA Tattoo artist**," "Looking for **Pittsburgh Steeler Jerseys**? Steeler Town has got 'em all."

And you want to weave them in so that the text still reads like human beings wrote it.

If I was trying to include "Denver tax preparer" in my "about" section, I might do something like: "*John Smith is a dedicated Denver tax preparer whose sole mission is to help people reach their financial goals, build for their economic future and defraud the IRS.*"

Quick Tip: Don't forget to include your website in the very first part of your "About" Section. This is the most visible area for you to include a link on your Facebook Fan Page. And can lead to lots of additional traffic back to your own website.

FAN-PAGE SEO HACK NO. 3: BUILD YOUR PAGE SOME BACKLINK LOVE

We talked about backlinks earlier, how they don't work quite as well as they used to and have been seriously devalued by Big, Bad Google.

But they work devastatingly well for Fan Pages. Mostly because nobody ever thinks to send backlinks to their Facebook page.

So, here's what you do:

- ☑ **Decide on 3-5 keywords that are relevant to your business.** At least three words long.

- ☑ **Head over to Fiverr.com to purchase a couple of "SEO gigs."** Sort by "rating" to find the most reliable freelancers.

- ☑ **Purchase three gigs, $15 total,** and have the freelancer build some backlinks to the URL of your Fan Page, using those 3-5 keywords.

This won't suddenly change things overnight. But slowly you'll find your Fan Page beating well-established websites in the search-engine rankings. (Not bad for the price of a Taylor Swift CD.)

CHAPTER 1 KEY TAKEAWAYS:

☑ Insert a keyword in your Facebook name. (But don't go overboard.)

☑ Put your keywords in your Facebook page about section, description, short description, company overview, mission, and products field.

☑ Go to Fiverr.com and hire some freelancers to hook you up with some backlinks.

Chapter 2:

The Ultimate Facebook Fan Page Makeover

"The power of finding beauty in the humblest of things makes home happy and life lovely."

-Louisa May Alcott

I wish I could tell you looks don't matter. But we both know that's not true.

How your Facebook Fan Page looks — how cool, fun and relevant to your audience your page appears to be — makes a huge difference in the success of your Facebook marketing.

So before we start getting likes and fans and (more importantly) customers, we're going to need to pimp out our Facebook fan page to make it sleek, modern and one kick-ass lead-generatin' machine.

So, here's my THREE Step Facebook Makeover checklist to help your Fan page look like you spent thousands of dollars getting it designed, for just the price of a triple grande latte:

FAN PAGE MAKEOVER STEP NO. 1: CREATE A TIMELINE COVER PHOTO THAT DOESN'T SUCK

I don't usually encourage folks to spend a ton of time on the creative for their social media profiles.

But Facebook is different.

So much of the real estate on your Facebook fan page is devoted to photos. (Facebook isn't stupid, they know most people are lazy and hate to read anything more than a sentence or two.)

There is one particular photo you need to worry about. And that's the Timeline cover photo.

The Timeline Cover Photo is the one at the very top of your fan page that stretches horizontally over the entire width of your page.

And it's really important.

It's your very own billboard, except you can't put in contact info, arrows, references to likes or shares, or any kind of call to action.

But that doesn't mean you can't do some serious marketing damage with this space. Here are some tips to crush it with your Timeline Photo:

☑ **Use a photo-heavy design that incorporates the vibe of your company**. And by vibe, I don't mean your boring conference room. What is the mission of your company; what feelings do you hope to convey to your customers; what's the core benefit of your products or services?

☑ **Unless you have an inner graphic designer in you, hire an outside designer** to make this photo awesome and not sucky. oDesk (http://punkrockmarketing.com/odesk) and Elance (http://punkrockmarketing.com/elance) are great places to find talent for super cheap.

☑ **If you do have some design mojo in your DNA, crank up the saturation and contrast** in the photo to make your cover really pop. This can help take even the most dull, flat pics and make them look awesome.

☑ **Ideally, the cover photo should have pictures of people**.

Preferably you or people on your team are best, but attractive women are good too. (I know, sounds superficial. It is. And it works.) You just want to do more than show your logo. (Bo-ring!)

☑ **Pick warm colors (red, brown, orange).** Anything that contrasts with the LA Dodgers color scheme Facebook forces upon the world.

☑ **Unless your brand is instantly recognizable, include a tagline that tells us what your company does.** So your company is named Marketing Mojo, what the hell does that mean? If it's not clear from your company name, add a tagline, something like: "Training, Support, Solutions" or "Your Social Media Sherpa."

☑ **If relevant, add in testimonials (along with head shots) of your customers.** Social proof is HUGE. And having that baked in to your timeline photo can do absolute wonders.

☑ **Feel free to create a new cover photo for any upcoming promotions, events or product launches.** Got an upcoming webinar? Or a new mini-course you're teaching? Or maybe a live conference event you're organizing? Create a new cover photo to act as a billboard for your shiny new thing you're promoting.

FAN-PAGE MAKEOVER STEP NO. 2: CREATE A PROFILE PHOTO THAT DOESN'T SUCK

The profile photo is the small thumbnail in the Timeline Cover Photo, on the lower left-hand side. While it doesn't have the sheer "Look at Me, and All of This Cool Stuff I Can Sell You" potential that the Timeline cover photo does...

...it does have a valuable function.

It quickly separates you from the rest of the pack in your fans' newsfeeds. (And most of the time your fans will see this 90% more than they do your timeline cover photo.)

So here are some best practices when it comes to creating a killer profile pic:

☑ **Start with a quality photo**. Sounds like a no-brainer. But I'm still shocked by how many people use a less-than-stellar pic for their profile spot.

☑ **Go with a shot of a person, if you can**. Unless you're a huge company, I always recommend going with a headshot over a brand logo. (You're trying to sneak into the news feed, and logos scream "I'm a business who wants you to buy stuff.")

☑ **When in doubt, go with images over words**. This profile pic will eventually be sized down to 160x160px, so if you can't see your verbiage at that size, remove it from the picture altogether.

☑ **Don't keep changing your profile pic**. The timeline cover photo can/should be changed frequently. But once you hone in on a good profile pic, stick with it.

FAN-PAGE MAKEOVER STEP NO. 3: ADD YOUR
GREATEST HITS TO YOUR TIMELINE

Everyone loves a good success story. And that includes your Facebook fans.

For some unknown reason, people like to scroll through fan pages to find out about the history of a company. (Sounds terribly boring to me, but trust me, people do this.)

And not only that, but these milestones can be a great way to send traffic back to your own website.

So, it behooves you to take a few minutes to brainstorm 10 or so key milestones for your company.

These could include:

☑ The day your company opened its doors.

☑ The day your company reached a certain profit threshold.

☑ The day your company served a famous (ish) person, or a specific-numbered customer.

☑ Products or services you launched.

☑ Key partnerships you entered into or huge contracts you were a part of.

☑ Employees who joined the team.

☑ Awards your company won.

☑ Special events your business was a part of.

☑ Key events in your local community. (Charity stuff works really well here.)

So, what do you do when you've got your list of "milestones?" Well, here's what I do:

☑ **Find a LARGE photo that corresponds to the milestone.** 843 px x 403 px is the ideal size for these milestone pics, so BIGGER is always BETTER.

☑ **Add your milestone to your Fan Page Timeline.** To do this, just click on "Offer/Event" in the status update bar of your page, and then select milestone. (Include a keyword, if you can, in the event or story fields.)

☑ **Add a CTA (call-to-action) in the "Story" field.** (Example: Here's a picture from my first seminar. (When I had more hair.) To check out our brand new marketing seminars, head over to http://coolwebsite.com/seminars.)

CHAPTER 2 KEY TAKEAWAYS:

☑ Create a quality and warm-colored Timeline cover photo that captures the vibe of your company.

☑ Have your profile picture be a quality photo of a real person and don't change it, unless you think you can improve upon it.

☑ Create a "greatest hits" on your Facebook Timeline and be sure to incorporate corresponding photos and stories.

Chapter 3:

Facebook Apps (Where the REAL Money Is)

"There is no one giant step that does it. It's a lot of little steps."

-Peter A. Cohen

Like most things with Facebook, apps can be really confusing.

First of all, they are NOTHING like your smartphone apps. (Another instance in which Facebook doesn't know how to name things.)

Facebook apps are really just a fancy way of describing the custom tabs (small rectangles) that lie just below your Timeline cover photo. (The first one you always see is the Photos App.)

I'm not going to go into the whole technical side of how Facebook apps work. (It's boring and not that important for you to know.)

Just know this about Facebook custom apps:

☑ **Facebook really, really, really doesn't want its users to leave the Facebook universe**. Kinda like that creepy person who keeps texting you over and over.

☑ **Custom apps are a way for businesses to bring THEIR website INTO the Facebook universe**. As long as that business follows Facebook's strict terms of service.

☑ **Setting up Facebook custom apps is rather technical, and best left to the pro**s. It involves code and a heavy dose of caffeine.

☑ **Custom apps are ABSOLUTELY the best way to turn fans into customer**s. And also the best way to utilize a Facebook ad budget, which we'll dig into further in Chapter 6.

So, here are my FOUR Tips for Making the Most of Your Facebook Custom Apps:

FACEBOOK APP TIP NO. 1: ADD SOCIAL NETWORKS TO YOUR FAN PAGE

If you've got a presence on one of the other social networks, like Twitter or Pinterest, then it's a good idea to add a custom app that pulls in that content into your Facebook page.

The place I go to create these apps is WooBox (http://woobox.com). It's FREE and you can create custom apps for your YouTube channel, Twitter feed, Instagram profile, Pinterest account and bunch of other cool social networks.

They even offer a bunch of cool apps for contests and sweepstakes you may want to run. (Although I have another service I use for those. We'll dig deeper into contests in Chapter 7.)

I've dabbled with all of these, but the ones I've had the biggest success with are the YouTube and Pinterest apps. Facebook users love visual stuff, and those two networks do an amazing job of catering to the whole ADD Facebook crowd.

Facebook App Tip No. 2: Move All That Facebook Crap Out of the Way

Okay, so take a look at your page. You should see the "photos" custom app in the #1 spot.

There's nothing you can do about that app. It's like my mother's dedication to Fox News Channel: rock-solid, and never likely to change.

But next to that, if you haven't moved it already, is the *Thumbs up Like button app*.

And while that app may appeal to your vanity, it's precious real estate wasted. I HIGHLY recommend you move that puppy down the line, and get it out of the Top 4 spots. (The first four custom apps are the ones visitors see without hitting the "more" button.)

How do you move the apps? Simple…

1. Click on the "down arrow" button to the right of the apps.
2. Click on the "pencil" icon in the upper-right hand corner of the app you want to move.
3. Select which app you'd like to "swap position with."

Facebook App Tip No. 3: Create an Email Capture App

So I'm gonna assume you have some kind of email autoresponder service that can help you capture email addresses and blast out emails to new subscribers. (I cover this in more depth in Part Five of this book.)

If you don't, I highly recommend the autoresponder service AWeber — for a $1 trial head over to http://punkrockmarketing.com/aweber — but there are a ton of other services which are also good, such as InfusionSoft.

No matter what your business model, having a list of email

addresses you can continue to market to is worth its weight in Gmail gold.

But you still run into the problem of how to get those Facebook fans over to your email opt-in forms on your website.

Well, that's why you need a landing page tab on your Facebook page that collects all those email addresses.

There are essentially two ways to do this:

1. **The DIY method**. This involves having an SSL certificate, a developer app, integration with your webhost. (Total pain.)

2. **Get PageModo** (http://pagemodo.com) to do it for you. (For FREE!)

I'll let you guess which method I prefer.

If you really want to give your inner coder a try, here is a link to a thorough tutorial (http://punkrockmarketing.com/fbooktutorial) on how to do it.

But if you want to save your brain for other important details, like making sure your business stays solvent, then head over to PageModo (http://pagemodo.com) to have them worry about the technical details. (They can even design the custom app for you. Pretty cool.)

Yes, it'll cost you a bit of money to get the fancier features. But it's totally worth it not to have to learn what the hell an SSL certificate is, and why Facebook is so anal about it.

Facebook App Tip No. 4:
Create a Product Sales App

You can do a heck of a lot more than just create email capture pages on your Fan page. You can also SELL your stuff right there on Facebook. (Supremely handy.)

Virtually anything you can create on your website — shopping carts, video players, slide bars, interactive games, maps, coupons — can be replicated on Facebook. As long as you know what you're doing.

Again, I defer to the smart creative types over at PageModo. I use them for all my custom apps and have seen a huge boost in my profits as a result.

Bonus: Creating all these custom apps will SAVE you a ton of money when it comes to creating Facebook ads, of which we'll cover more in-depth in Chapter 6.

CHAPTER 3 Key Takeaways:

☑ Go to WooBox to create a custom app that will allow you to add other social networks to your Fan Page.

☑ Move the Thumps up Like button app and other apps that take a lot of real estate down on your Fan Page.

☑ Use PageModo to create an email capture app on your Fan Page.

☑ Get PageModo to also create a product sales app on your Fan Page.

Chapter 4:

7 Secrets to Facebook Engagement Awesomeness

"Our chief want is someone who will inspire us to be what we know we could be."

-Ralph Waldo Emerson

Okay, here's where we really dig into the trenches of Facebook Marketing.

This is where we answer such eternal questions as…

☑ What the hell am I going to post on my Facebook Page?

☑ When is the best TIME to post?

☑ How do we attract the largest audience possible with our posts? (Ie: Get fans to share stuff for us because we're too lazy to do it ourselves.)

☑ How do I make sure I don't waste my time with all this posting crap?

All the tips I'm going to share in this chapter have been tested and discovered the hard way. (Meaning I tried a bunch of other things that didn't work at all, until I accidentally tried this stuff and it worked.)

But before we get into the nitty-gritty, let me share with you three key things I've learned about posting stuff on Facebook Fan Pages that I think will really help:

1. It's NOT about you.
2. People really LIKE to feel important.
3. It's NOT about you.

For years I thought my fans wanted authenticity, connections, personal narratives, information and a feeling of community.

Nope.

They want to feel smart and get FREE stuff. (Everything else is just frosting.)

So, here are my SEVEN Secrets to Killer Facebook Fan-Page Posting:

SECRET NO. 1: PHOTOS, ALWAYS PHOTOS

I'm not going to bore you with the stats, except…okay… maybe I'll bore you a little.

According to HubSpot, photos on Facebook generate 53% more likes and 104% more comments than the average post. (In case your math skills are a bit shaky, this is a lot.)

So, it doesn't matter if you're linking to a blog post you wrote, or sharing a favorite quote of yours or telling people about this cool YouTube video you found…

…find a RELEVANT photo that goes along with your post. (And upload it right along with your post.)

Even if the thing you're sharing is already pulling a thumbnail photo, I want you to upload a photo anyway. (It could be a screenshot of the webpage or a stock photo that is somehow related. Whatever. Just get a photo up there with it.)

Cool thing is, if you have a photo, then you can also upload to it your Pinterest feed when you're done uploading it to Facebook.

SECRET NO. 2: ASK QUESTIONS, PLAY GAMES, INSPIRE FOLKS

The best, and I mean the absolute best, results I get from status updates all seem to revolve around some question or game that my fans can't help but answer.

A couple of my go-to examples of this would include:

☑ Fill-in-the-blank. "My favorite horror movie is ___?"

☑ Simple, easy questions. ("What's your favorite candy bar?")

☑ Write a caption to a photo.

☑ Trivia questions.

☑ Motivational Quotes. ("The secret to getting ahead is getting started." -Mark Twain…Do you agree?")

☑ How many ___ can you find in this picture?

☑ What's your biggest frustration/gripe about ___?

☑ What's one word that describes ___?

I know. Sounds like games you play with kindergarteners.

That's. The. Point.

You are (most likely) talking to people who are scanning your page on their phone while they're on the toilet.

No in-depth questions about congressional law or macroeconomics. Simple, breezy, fun.

SECRET NO. 3: END EVERY POST WITH A QUESTION

You'll notice in the above example, the one with the Mark Twain quote, that I added a "Do you agree?" at the end?

This is key to boosting your engagement, and your likelihood of showing up, not only in your fans' newsfeed, but in their friend's feed as well. (This is how you get huge exposure, really fast.)

So it doesn't matter if you're sharing a video of Sarah Palin next to a decapitated turkey or a dissertation on Soviet history, always give some kind of directive to your readers to comment and get involved, which could be one of the following:

☑ Do you agree?

☑ Click "Like" if you agree

☑ Have you had trouble with _____?

☑ Have you had success with _____?

☑ What do you think?

Secret No. 4: Ask People to Share Your Stuff

I'm always surprised this works. I mean people aren't lemmings. They aren't robots that you just tell what to do.

They are critical-thinking, sentient beings who have a mind of their own.

Yeah, well, not on Facebook they don't. The stats are startling:

☑ Seven times more engagement when you ask people to "share" a post.

☑ 3.3 times more engagement when you ask people to "comment."

☑ Just using the words like, caption, share, or thumbs up can lead to 48 percent more shares.

Don't wait for people to magically "share" your stuff. Ask them to do so. (And they'll probably do it.)

SECRET NO. 5: KEEP IT SHORT

This one also shocked me. I mean, surely, the more you put in your posts the more that people would respond.

Yeah...not so much.

Turns out, from the folks at Buddy Media, posts with 80 characters or less had 23% more interaction.

Just so you know, that's damn short.

The answer to why this is so, may be in another statistic: 75 percent of all Facebook posts are longer than 80 characters.

That means if you want to stand out, and get noticed in the newsfeed, keep it short and keep it simple. (Because your competition sure has hell ain't.)

SECRET NO. 6: POST IN THE EVENINGS AND ON THE WEEKENDS

Unlike Twitter, which practically goes into a coma when the sun goes down, Facebook is still blocked by many workplaces.

Which means weekends and weekday evenings are the prime Facebook times.

Now this may change, as we all shift toward even more mobile consumption, but I can speak from personal experience: I find the posts with the largest number of comments, likes and shares happen in the evenings and on weekends.

But it'll depend on your business. So, here are a couple guidelines to keep you straight:

☑ **If you're a restaurant, post in the morning and just after lunch**. Especially if you post coupons and special offers on your Facebook page.

☑ **If you're in any kind of retail, 8-5 will probably be your sweet spot**. Again, especially if you're offering a deal.

☑ **For everyone else, I would suggest you focus on the following must-post times**: a) Weekday evenings (about 7:30 pm, local time) b) Saturday mornings c) Sunday mornings d) Sunday evenings e) Weekday lunch time (avoid Fridays)

Note: Don't take my word for it. If you're selling network solutions, then maybe late afternoon on the east coast of America is your best time. Try some times out and see what works for you.

SECRET NO. 7: POST 4-7 TIMES A WEEK (MAKE A SCHEDULE)

I know. You're busy. Posting five times a week sounds like Medieval torture.

But, here's the thing, if you ain't gonna do it at least 4-7 times a week, then you may not want to spend a ton of time doing it at all.

Facebook not only rewards likes and shares but also "freshness." And if your Facebook content has been sitting out on the counter for a while and starts to go bad, it'll be hard for any of your posts to get much traction.

The key to making this work, especially if you have ZERO TIME to spare, is to create a calendar you can work off.

Something like:

☑ Monday: Motivational Quote
☑ Tuesday: Fill in the Blank
☑ Wednesday: Quick Tip of The Week
☑ Thursday: Caption Contest
☑ Friday: Fan Spotlight

☑ Saturday: Promotional (Something Related to Your Business)

☑ Sunday: Video Tip of the Week

Now, you don't have to follow my calendar. At all.

But if you set up some kind of template to work off, it'll make it much easier to come up with stuff to post.

Bonus: Having a schedule makes it much easier to outsource your Facebook Page updating. (Hint, hint.)

CHAPTER 4 Key Takeaways:

☑ Try to always post photos, since they generate more buzz.

☑ Entice your readership with quotes, games and easy questions.

☑ Always ask questions. Always.

☑ Ask people to share your stuff.

☑ Try to keep your posts short, ideally fewer than 80 characters.

☑ Depending on your business, try to post during times you think you will receive the most engagement.

☑ Create a post schedule and try to post at least once a day.

Chapter 5:

How to Get Thousands of Fans (Without Hardly Trying)

"Only one man in a thousand is a leader of men — the other 999 follow women."

-Groucho Marx

All the inspirational quotes and pictures of kittens and bunnies on your Facebook Page Timeline won't do you much good if there are no eyeballs to see them.

But like a junior high school dance where all the students are too scared to be the first one on the dance floor, sometimes you've got to scrape and claw for your first 100 or so fans, so the rest of the universe thinks your page is worth "liking."

So, here are SIX (FREE) techniques to boost your fanbase overnight:

SUPER-QUICK FAN STRATEGY NO. 1: LEAVE YOUR FACEBOOK FOOTPRINT EVERYWHERE

And I mean everywhere. This could include:

☑ Your email signature

☑ Your forum or message board signature and/or profile

☑ Other social network profiles (Such as Twitter, YouTube, Pinterest, etc.)

☑ At the end of every blog post your write. Whether on your site or on somebody else's site.

☑ In the description of every YouTube video you upload.

☑ At your store's front counter.

☑ On your employees' t-shirts.

☑ Any direct mail or offline promo materials.

☑ Ad Media Buys, such as TV, radio, print, or online.

And how do you get people to follow you? Could be something as simple as using the following verbiage:

☑ Follow Us on Facebook for Special Offers

☑ Follow Us on Facebook for Tips and Tutorials

☑ Follow us on Facebook for Members-Only Coupons

☑ Follow Us on Facebook for Members-Only Content

Whatever it is, you want to make people feel like they're getting something for following you. (Besides boosting your self-esteem.)

Super-Quick Fan Strategy No. 2: Add facebook
ICONS TO YOUR WEBSITE

This one SHOULD be a no-brainer, right? But so many marketers screw this up.

I think that's because Facebook makes the entire "liking" experience so damn confusing.

People can "like" your blog post, but not necessarily "like" your Page.

They can "like" a comment, but not "like" the blog post itself. (Only Mark Zuckerberg could make me "hate" the word "like" so very much.)

Here's the deal, there are two prominent areas on your website or blog that you want to have Facebook icon placement:

1) A FACEBOOK "LIKE" BOX ON THE SIDEBAR OF YOUR WEBSITE.

These are one of those cool-looking square boxes that: a) encourages visitors to follow you on Facebook b) shows them how many fans you have c) shows them how many of those fans are their own friends and d) gives them a chance to "like" your page without leaving your website.

This is the absolute #1 way to get new fans from visitors who frequent your website.

To install this like box, just head over to the Facebook Like Box Developer Page (http://punkrockmarketing.com/like-box). They've got some, surprisingly, straightforward documentation there to help.

You basically just:

☑ Create the like box plugin on the Facebook developer page.

☑ Insert the code into the sidebar of your website. If you're using WordPress there are plugins that specifically do this. Otherwise you can find a developer-for-hire on Fiverr. com to help.

2) Add Facebook Comments to Your Blog Posts and/or Web Articles

Want immediate and instant feedback to the stuff you publish on your website? (I know. Scary, right?)

Don't worry, the possible downside to hearing brutal feedback from your visitors is greatly outweighed by the awesomeness of having comments on your website, show up in your visitors' — and their friends'the revelation — newsfeed. (Talk about viral.)

Just another in a long line of reasons to ensure your website content has killer titles that catch the attention of people who have no idea who you are.

To add comments to your site, just check out, again, this Facebook Developers Comments page for instructions on how to do it. (http://punkrockmarketing.com/commentsbox)

Super-Quick Fan Strategy No. 3: Beg Your Friends to Like Your Page

This one may sound pathetic, but it totally works.

Considering the average Facebook user has an average of about 240 friends, asking your existing (personal) Facebook network to "like" your page can be the quickest way to boost that fan total, especially for a brand new page.

What I usually do is make an appeal that is whimsical and self-deprecating at the same time:

"Hey guys!

"I just created this awesome, amazing new Facebook Page that will completely revolutionize the entire world, and quite possibly save civilization. Unfortunately we've only got three fans so far. (One of them is my mother.)

"Will you help us out by clicking 'like' and becoming a fan? A grateful nation thanks you."

Feel free to leave out the part about your mother. Otherwise, the rest of it works pretty well. (Don't be pushy or obnoxious.)

Super-Quick Fan Strategy No. 4: Like (and Interact) With Other Facebook Pages

Here's something you might not know. The more pages you like, the more people will see your profile picture and come into contact with your page.

Obviously, it helps to choose fan pages whose fanbase would make for ideal customers. And if you go a step further, by commenting and chatting with folks, you can attract even more fans. (Especially if what you have to say isn't totally inane and annoying.)

How do you do this? Simple:

- ☑ Go to your page.
- ☑ In the upper right hand corner, next to the "Home" button you'll see (most likely) a thumbnail of your personal profile.
- ☑ Click on the image.
- ☑ You'll see an option to "Use Facebook as…"
- ☑ Scroll down until you see your page.
- ☑ Choose the page you want to use…and start surfing the Facebook universe as your Fan Page.

SUPER-QUICK FAN STRATEGY NO.5: PUT A "FOLLOW US" LINK ON YOUR THANK YOU PAGES

Once somebody has bought something from you, or has opted into your email list, they are what you might refer to as a "hot lead."

So why not add them to your Facebook tribe at the same time? (And possibly keep selling to them in different ways over and over again.)

To add some "Follow Us" code, just head over to the Facebook Developer Follow Button page (http://punkrockmarketing.com/followbutton), put in your website info and drop the code into your website.

SUPER-QUICK FAN STRATEGY NO. 6: BUY SOME LIKES

I know. You shouldn't have to "pay" for people to "like" your page.

Yeah, well, books about moody teenage vampires shouldn't become the most profitable book series of all time. But things happen.

And, if you find you're not getting a ton of fans quick enough, then you may need to expend a little bit of cash to boost your fanbase.

Now, we're going to cover Facebook ads more extensively in Chapter 6, but for now realize that for a couple bucks a day you can create some pretty ninja Facebook engagement ads that can quite accurately target the people who are most likely to purchase your products and services.

In the biz, these are called "Click Like" ads, so named for that oft-used way they are presented. ("Click Like if You'd Rather Be at the Racetrack," "Click Like If you Love Romance

Novels," "Click Like if You Believe Facebook is Spying on You...RIGHT NOW!")

What's key with these types of ads is you are not "selling" your fan page. You are selling the "click" or the "like." (Much easier, and cheaper than other forms of Facebook advertising as well.)

CHAPTER 5   KEY TAKEAWAYS:

☑ Link back to your Fan Page everywhere and offer people something so they will follow you.

☑ Put your Facebook icons on your website and/or blog and add Facebook comments to your blog posts or web articles for instant feedback.

☑ Beg your friends to like your Fan Page.

☑ Use your Fan Page to like and comment on other Pages.

☑ Create a "Follow Us" link on your thank you pages.

☑ Use "Click Like" ads to boost your fanbase.

Chapter 6:

Facebook Advertising for Fun (and Massive Profit)

"The purpose of business is to create and keep a customer."

-Peter F. Drucker

As much as I hate Facebook pages and profiles and like buttons and comment boxes…

…I LOVE Facebook advertising.

That's because Facebook ads:

☑ Are way cheaper than Google Adwords ads.

☑ Gets way, way more traffic than ad platforms such as Bing or other independent ad networks.

☑ Can be targeted by precise — and I mean precise — interests, gender, location, place of work, and any number of super targeted methods.

☑ Are a fantastic, cheap way to ensure your content gets seen by a ton of people.

☑ Are done poorly by most other marketers. (Including your competition.)

Now, Facebook advertising does have a lot of components to it. And I'm only going to have room here to give you an in-depth overview and some of the insider tips and strategies that I follow.

If you'd like a real Ph.D. education in Facebook Ads, let me suggest checking out my colleague, and fellow San Diego resident, Amy Porterfield's online course called FB Influence (http://punkrockmarketing.com/fbinfluence).

Amy wrote the book Facebook for Dummies, and has worked with diverse peeps such as Tony Robbins and Harley Davidson. FB Influence is a highly recommended addition to your business library.

Okay, enough of the spiel. Let's dive into Facebook ads.

WHY YOU SHOULD CARE ABOUT FACEBOOK ADS

As you'll soon find out, there are quite a few different kinds of Facebook ads. (And they all have eerily-similar names which makes things even more confusing.)

But all ads have at least one of the following goals tied to them:

- ☑ To get a visitor to "like" your page.
- ☑ To get a visitor to check out your custom app. (Where you can have them sign up for your email list or have them buy something from you.)
- ☑ To make a specific post on your page more visible to a fan, or friend of your fan.
- ☑ To make a specific post on your page more visible to a non-fan.
- ☑ To promote an event, offer, coupon, local business, product, or program to fans and non-fans alike.
- ☑ To get a visitor to leave Facebook and check out your own website.

Of the above goals, I would avoid the last one. Not only are those ads more expensive, but they don't perform very well. (Facebook is like a candy store. People just don't like to leave unless there's something else really enticing.)

So now that we know a little bit about what we can do with ads, let's dig into the different ad formats, and find out which ones are the best to help you reach your goals.

FACEBOOK AD TYPE No.1: EXTERNAL WEBSITE (MARKETPLACE) ADS

These are the ads that have been around Facebook since the beginning of time. (Or at least 2009.)

They can usually be found on the right side of a user's Facebook interface, and they are most often used to send traffic to an external (your) website.

Specs:

☑ Image: 99x72px

☑ 90 character limit

☑ Title of Ad: Whatever you choose

Pros:

☑ Best for sending direct traffic to your own off-Facebook web location.

☑ Nothing else I can think of.

Cons:

☑ Most expensive type of ad.

☑ Most users have "banner blindness" to them.

☑ Hard to get these types of ads approved.

Copy Example:

☑ "Looking for a New…(Bank, Realtor, Fishing Reel, Karate Instructor, etc.)? Check out our amazing, wonderful thing/widget that will transform your life and bring meaning to your pitiful existence. Supplies limited, call now!"

Facebook Ad Type No.2: Click "Like" Ads

These ads are also displayed on the right side as well, but unlike the External ads, and my twelve year-old nephew, they can do two things at once.

They can:

a. Allow people to "like" your ad without clicking on it (in the form of a small thumb like icon below the photo of the ad).

b. Send visitors who click on the ad to a Facebook page, custom app, or event.

For the most part, this one is really about driving traffic to a specific Facebook page that boosts your bottom line. Whatever you do, don't send people to your Fan Page home page or the timeline with these ads. That's a waste of money.

Specs:

☑ Image: 99x72px

☑ 90 character limit

☑ Title of Ad: The name of your page. (Sorry, no flexibility here.)

Pros:

- ☑ Awesome ability to have people "like" your page AND click over to your specified destination at the same time.

- ☑ Good way to go after a narrowly-targeted audience.

- ☑ Great way to send people to a landing page that is similar to a landing page that is already converting on your own website.

Cons:

- ☑ Ad is placed on right-hand side. (May not get discovered.)

- ☑ More expensive than other forms of Facebook ads. (Especially if your targeting is very specific.)

Copy Example:

- ☑ "Click Like if You'd Rather Be…(Reading Twilight, Doing Yoga, Deep Sea Diving, Not Using Facebook, etc.) Right Now."

FACEBOOK AD TYPE No.3: PAGE POST ADS

These type of ads take existing content on your Fan Page — whether it be a photo, video, text, link, question, or whatever — and turn it into an ad.

These are really good for engagement; they are the most social type of ads you can get and, at a relatively cheap price, they are a great addition to your ad toolbox. Another bonus to these is that they boost your affinity score fast, which can make your other ad campaigns cheaper.

Suffice it to say, I use this type of ad a lot.

Specs:

☑ Image-Pulled from post. (Ideal size is 400x300 pixels)

☑ 120 character limit, after which the post is truncated. (So you'll want to make sure your post's text doesn't ramble.)

☑ Title of Ad: Pulled from post

Pros:

☑ Can be targeted to anyone. (Fans, non-fans, friends of fans, the Pope, whoever!)

☑ Non-fans of your page can "like" your page directly from the ad.

☑ These ads appear in a user's newsfeeds.

☑ They are also one of the few ads that shows up on mobile devices. (Huge!)

☑ Sneaky…they don't look like ads.

☑ Much higher CTR (Click-Thru-Rate) and lower CPC (Cost-Per-Click) than External ads.

Cons:

☑ Doesn't send traffic to a landing page. Just sends traffic to your post.

☑ Doesn't do you much good if you're not able to eventually convert fans into leads.

☑ Without a decent picture and a catchy post title, this type of ad probably won't work for you.

Copy Examples:

☑ World Premiere video: Justin Timberlake debates the merits of Congress on C-SPAN.

☑ 30% off July 1-5. Connect with Bass and Pro Shop for an additional 10% off stuff we couldn't sell.

☑ Does your Facebook marketing strategy blow? In this blog post, Michael from Punk Rock Marketing shows you how not to suck so badly.

Facebook Ad Type No. 4: Sponsored Stories

Okay, here's where it starts to get confusing.

You'd assume with a name like "sponsored stories" that this would be about promoting a specific "story" on your Fan Page.

Yeah, you'd be wrong.

A better way to describe this type of ad is to call it a "Sneaky User Endorsement." Where the actions of your fans are suddenly made very public to their own friends.

These actions can include:

☑ Pages and posts they've liked

☑ Posts they've commented on

☑ Places they've checked in to

☑ Games they've played; apps they've used

☑ Events they've signed up for

No doubt you've seen these ads probably, and thought: "Okay…so my loser cousin just played 'Mafia Wars.' Why should I care and why am I seeing this now?"

You're seeing it, because Mafia Wars paid for you to see it.

These can be very effective ads, but I wouldn't advise you to start off with these types of ads. (Get a few campaigns under your belt, and dig in when you're feeling more comfortable with the Facebook ad dashboard.)

Specs:

☑ Image: Pulled from thumbnail of user and your Page Profile pic

☑ Text is limited "Lady Gaga likes Fox News"…so character limit is irrelevant.

☑ Title of Ad: N/A

Pros:

☑ Very interactive ad. If you have a decent fan base, this is a really effective way to boost your number of fans.

☑ Social proof element is very, very strong.

☑ Works best with fun(ish) business models. (Does your friend "liking" a CPA firm get you to take action? I'm not so sure.)

☑ Great for app and game developers.

☑ Great conversation starter.

☑ Awesome for an event, especially in the weeks leading up to it.

☑ Can target specifically where ad shows up (mobile, desktop, newsfeed).

Cons:

☑ Complicated. Lots of options.

☑ Doesn't lend itself immediately to a huge ROI (return on investment).

☑ No control over the creative of the ad.

Copy Example:

☑ Michael Rogan just…(voted for the next American Idol; claimed on offer from Macy's; liked the San Diego

Chargers post; checked in at Darth Vader's Throne Room on the Death Star; etc.)

Facebook Ad Type No.5: Promoted Posts

Confused yet? Don't worry, after this you will be. (I swear it took me months to get the difference between promoted posts and page post ads.)

Promoted posts are (somewhat) like Page Post ads in that you are promoting a specific item you've shared on Facebook (status update, photo, video, questions, offers, your favorite Justin Bieber album…)

But unlike Page Post ads, you don't get all that cool niche targeting; you can only show promoted posts to fans and friends of fans.

But…

You do get a much cheaper ad price, and these are really ideal for targeting mobile users because these promoted posts show up in the FEED, not in the Facebook Siberia on the right navigation of the page.

Read that again: these are superb for reaching people on their mobile phone. (If you don't think that's important, you're crazy.)

Unfortunately, you have to have 400 likes before you can use promoted posts, but once you do reach that threshold, this can be a super cheap way to ensure your important updates and promotions reach the biggest number of fans possible.

Specs:
☑ Image: Pulled from post

Pros:

☑ Great way to build engagement (which can affect your ad spend for other ad types).

☑ Can target friends of fans. (Super-key, especially if your business is locally or interest-based.)

☑ Only runs for three days, so not a huge expenditure.

☑ Great for mobile. Gotta say it again…your ad shows up IN the feed.

Cons:

☑ Only runs for three days, so you can't continue to run a successful campaign.

☑ Proves that the model going forward for Facebook is to have all status updates on a pay-to-play basis. (If you don't pay, nobody will ever see your stuff.)

Copy Example:

☑ The…(fedora, bow tie, "Star Wars" suspenders, etc.). Classically elegant, and never goes out of style. How do you wear it?

FACEBOOK AD TYPE NO. 6: FACEBOOK OFFERS, CONTESTS, AND PROMOTIONS

So, I know these aren't technically ads…but who are we kidding? These are some of the most effective forms of Facebook advertising you can implement.

Because of that, I've given them their own chapter. (Yeah, they are that awesome.) So head over to Chapter 7 to get the straight scoop on Facebook offers and promotions.

But just so we don't get confused, here's how I break things down:

☑ If I'm promoting something that has a tangible benefit to the user (like a 50% off coupon, free online training, or buy one, get one offer), a Facebook offer or promotion is the way to go.

☑ If I'm trying to ramp up the engagement and traffic to a specific Facebook post or custom landing page, or if I'm focusing on lead generation or sending people directly to a sales page on my website, or I just want to use peer pressure and social proof to reach a really huge amount of new prospects...then the Page Post, Sponsored Story, Promoted Post, Externals, and Click Like Ad are all ad types I use in my marketing mix.

CHAPTER 6 KEY TAKEAWAYS:

☑ Facebook has five kinds of ads: 1) External Website Ads that link directly to your site 2) Click "like" Ads that allow people to both "like" your ad and click on it to go to your destination page 3) Page Post Ads take existing content on your Fan Page and turn it into an ad 4) Sponsored Stories are ads that reveal the actions of your fans to their own friends 5) Promoted Posts promote shared items to fans and friends of fans and are most effective for mobile-users.

☑ Don't forget about Facebook offers, contests, and promotions...but more on that later.

Chapter 7:

Contests, Offers and Events... Oh My!

"If you don't set goals, you can't regret not reaching them."

-Yogi Berra

Okay, we're finally here. This might be the most profitable part of this book.

Because this is where we leverage all the hard work we've done up to this point and create some rather cheap and easy customer funnels that directly affect our bottom line.

But you gotta do the prep work.

You have to build your Fan Page and post regular, frequent content that gets people to answer insipid questions and offer their opinions on a variety of subjects...

...so that when you do pull the trigger on these special promotions, your ad spends are low and your engagement is high and your fans don't feel like you're selling to them.

They just feel like it's a part of a conversation. And when you get that...you'll be amazed how much stuff you can sell.

So, let's dig right in and get started with the first pillar of my Trinity of Facebook Promotion Awesomeness, which is:

Facebook Promotion Awesomeness Pillar No. 1:
Contests and Sweepstakes

I'm still amazed by how popular Facebook contests are. (I don't get particularly jazzed about entering a photo contest to win a free smoothie, but I am not most people.)

For the most part, contests and sweepstakes can be an excellent way to build up your fanbase and spread the word about your product or service in no time.

But it helps to know the difference between a contest and a sweepstakes, and what you have to do with each of them, to comply with Facebook's terms of service.

Here's the scoop on *Sweepstakes*:

☑ **What They Are?** Chance-based promotions or random drawings usually hosted on a Facebook tab.

☑ **Do They Work?** Oh yeah. Especially if the prize is pretty cool.

☑ **How to Set Up?** Very easy to set up. Especially with a third-party sweepstakes app from a company such as WooBox or Wildfire, just fill in the fields and publish on a Facebook custom app.

☑ **What Info Do You Collect?** Entrants often fill out a single form, usually involving the submission of their name and email (and often location and a phone number for future text marketing).

☑ **Who to Target?** The barrier to entry for a sweepstakes should be quite low, which leads to a bigger pool of entrants. (Be aware, some people will enter more than once. Just the way it is.)

☑ **What Should the Prize Be?** Anything that is relevant to your fanbase. And cool!

Best practices:

☑ Keep the entry form simple and to the point.

☑ Have good pictures of the prize on your landing page.

☑ Choose a sweepstakes app that has mobile capabilities. (Sweepstakes spread super quickly through mobile devices.)

Contests, on the other hand, require a little bit more effort on the part of your fans, which can be good or bad. Here's the skinny on *Facebook Contests:*

☑ **What They Are?** Contests are promotions where entrants must perform a specific action (such as upload a photo, write a caption, shoot a video, make a comment, dash off a quick essay, etc.) to win a specified prize.

☑ **Do They Work?** Exceptionally well. When people go to the trouble of creating "something" for a contest, they often share it with all of their friends. (This stuff can spread REALLY fast.)

☑ **How to Set Up?** Just like a Facebook sweepstakes, you'll want to set up through a third-party app. Let them handle the technical and legal crap that goes with setting up a contest.

☑ **What Info Do You Collect?** Same as the sweepstakes. Name and email, at a minimum, and then location and phone number if you have a plan to use it. (Don't ask for more than that.)

☑ **Who to Target?** Whomever you think will actually take action and enter the contest. Will retirees in Phoenix upload their Instagram photos from your nightclub? Probably not. But goth teenagers might.

☑ **What Should the Prize Be?** Not only relevant, but something commensurate with the effort required for the contest. If you're asking people to write an essay, you need to offer them more than a Slurpee coupon.

Best practices:

☑ Make sure to create ads around your contests.

☑ Make the entry form SUPER CLEAR about what's needed to win. (Unclear contest guidelines can lead to huge headaches.)

☑ Like sweepstakes, make sure the app you use is mobile-friendly.

☑ All things being equal, go for photos over videos and captions over essays. (Make it easy and more people will enter.)

FACEBOOK PROMOTION AWESOMENESS PILLAR No. 2: OFFERS

I hate to break it to ya…but 57% of all Facebook users like a brand or company for the "discounts and offers" they receive.

That means, unless your Apple or Coke, your fans don't love your brand, they love a great deal.

Which is why Facebook offers are so frickin' awesome.

Here's how they work:

1. **Create an offer.** (Just click on the "offer/event" button in your status bar.)

2. **Promote your offer.** You can use many of the ad types we mentioned in the previous chapter, such as a Page Post ad, sponsored story or promoted post.

3. **Sit back and collect your money** as people redeem your offer.

One quick downside to Facebook offers is that you have to have 400 fans for your page before you can start using them. Otherwise these things totally rock.

So, what's so great about Facebook offers?

Well…

☑ You can choose whether people redeem them online or print them out and redeem them in person. (Ideal for online and local businesses alike.)

☑ The offer is tied to the email address that the user has connected to Facebook with. (This means they'll actually get it and use it!) And it won't be some spam filter email address.

☑ You can set a time limit for the offer.

☑ You can set up a quantity limit for the offer.

☑ If you promote with a page post ad, you can do some seriously cool location targeting.

☑ The offer can show up in the newsfeed for maximum visibility.

☑ Promoting your offer can be surprisingly cheap. (More on this later.)

What kinds of stuff can you promote with a Facebook offer? Obviously coupons and discounts work really well. But so do webinars, online trainings, video courses…pretty much anything where there is something of high perceived value being offered at some kind of special price.

Here are a couple of tips when crafting your Facebook offer to get the most bang for your buck:

☑ **Get to the point in your copy.** You've only got 90 characters so no futzing around talking about the features. Get right to the deal and what people can expect get from the deal. Example: "Click to receive 2-for-1 Pizza deal at New York Joe's."

☑ **Tell people to take action.** "Click here," "Click now,"

"Download now," "Grab yours now..." Don't be shy. Tell 'em what to do.

☑ **Set up an initial budget of about $30-$40 to get started.** This will get you a ton of exposure if your targeting is half-way decent.

☑ **Always opt for dollars saved, over percentage off.** Which sounds better: "50% off all blazers at Macy's," or "Save $20 on a Macy's blazer today"? Specific always beats vague.

FACEBOOK PROMOTION AWESOMENESS PILLAR NO. 3: EVENTS

If I'm being honest, I'm not a huge fan of Facebook events. Maybe it's because I don't actually care to be around people all that much.

That being said, Facebook events can be a great way to get a ton of people over to your offline, and online, events and eventually to sell them your stuff.

You just got to know what to do. (And what not to do.)

There are basically two components to successful Facebook events: creating events and promoting events.

But they are a little bit more complicated than Facebook offers, so here's a deep dive into the two-step process of how to set up your event:

STEP NO. 1: ADD THE EVENTS APP TO YOUR FACEBOOK PAGE

☑ Head over to your Facebook page and click on the "edit page" button.

☑ Click on the "update info" button.

☑ Click on the "apps" icon in the far left.

☑ Find the "events" app in the middle content section and select "Go to app."

STEP NO. 2: CREATE YOUR EVENT

☑ Write a description of your event (don't forget to include clear Calls-to-action in ALL CAPS).

☑ Fill in the time. (Don't forget your time zone; Facebook doesn't feel like that's important info and so leaves it out.)

☑ Specify where the event is. (Offline or online.)

☑ Uncheck the "Only admins can post to wall" feature; you want people to be able to discuss and ask questions.

☑ Add a killer image for your event.

So, now you've got your event created, how do you go about actually getting people to go to your event?

Well, here's my seven-step little formula for promoting an event:

1. Add the event to your timeline. (Don't forget the killer image and headline that screams "I want to attend!")

2. Create a brand new timeline cover photo (remember those?) that promotes the upcoming event.

3. Continually add videos, blog posts, updates, pictures from previous events — maybe a bit of coming attractions to your timeline.

4. Promote all of these assets with Promoted Posts.

5. "Tag" all the featured speakers or panel members in Facebook.

6. One week prior to the event, or when registration closes, promote your event with a Page Post Ad.

7. Promote your event everywhere else. (Twitter, Pinterest, Blog, LinkedIn, etc.)

CHAPTER 7 KEY TAKEAWAYS:

☑ Set up a sweepstakes or contest using Woobox, Wildfire or another 3rd party app that gives away a cool prize relevant to your business, and don't forget to make it mobile compatible.

☑ Create an offer and promote it through Facebook ads and make sure the offer gets to the point.

☑ Create an event by adding the event app on your Facebook Page and promote it through Facebook ads and any other social media website.

Epilogue:
If You Don't Like the
Weather...

You could spend months, if not years, trying to become a Facebook expert.

Don't.

It's not worth it.

The (somewhat) Draconian rules and regulations that Facebook forces upon its ~~victims~~ advertisers can be changed at any moment. (Without any warning.)

And that Fan Page community you've spent years cultivating can suddenly disappear because Facebook changed its quantum affinity alogrithm flux capacitor and you're left out in the Status Update cold.

And, though I have done my best to brain dump all the little ninja Facebook tricks and tactics I've learned the hard way (and at quite an expense)...the truth is that minutes after I finish typing this epilogue, some of the things in here may already be obsolete.

Just remember that as many new little tools and tweaks and "you gotta have this one thing" service Facebook offers...

...the principles will never change.

Facebook is that kid's tree house in the backyard.

It's a place where people like to meet up with their friends, catch up on gossip...even get into a couple of arguments.

But it's their place. Their zone. Their home away from the parents.

And it's your job as a Facebook marketer to build that tree house.

To fill it with comic books and Barbie dolls and baseball cards and an EZ Bake Oven, and let the kids just ramble on and have a great time and feel important and feel like this is the safest place in the world.

So, when you do have a product or service you think they'd like, or would enjoy, or could possibly improve/change their lives…

They'll pounce on it. Because they trust the tree house. (And the person who built it.)

And though I'm straining metaphors here a bit, I truly believe that (whether I like it or not) the only marketing that will survive in the competitive years ahead will be marketing that doesn't feel like marketing.

Selling that doesn't even remotely feel like selling.

Web properties that feel like tree houses.

Here's hoping this book provided a nail or two to help you build some tree houses for your business.

*   *   *

Freaked out by Facebook? Relaxxxxx…

To grab your very own FREE Facebook Marketing Cheat Sheet, head over to **PunkRockMarketing.com** TODAY and get instant access to your very own Facebook marketing checklist.

It's so easy, Mark Zuckerberg can do it without selling your data to advertisers.

Again, head over to PunkRockMarketing.com TODAY and get your FREE Facebook Marketing Cheat Sheet.

And if you have any questions, just drop me a line at Michael@punkrockmarketing.com.

Okay…now for something completely different (and pinworthy). It's time for…

Pinterest
MARKETING
THAT DOESN'T SUCK

Vol.4
of the Punk Rock
Marketing
COLLECTION

Michael Clarke

Prologue:
How I Stopped Hating Pinterest (and Started Making Money)

Pinterest is the Lady Gaga of social networks.

It's EITHER the hottest, hippest, most visually-engaging form of social media ever created, giving us a unique glimpse of what the **future** of online user behavior will look like OR...

...it's a one-hit wonder. A time suck for marketers NOT selling physical products NOT designed for women aged 21-45, and with its pinboards and likes and re-pins, offers little more than a pretty, shallow Facebook reboot.

And you know what?

They're both right. (IF you don't know what you're doing.)

Pinterest is, as the social media gurus claim, the ULTI-MATE marketing tool.

The FACT that Pinterest users will GLADLY share advertorial images of your product and services (with the price tag attached!) is worth more than a boatload of Facebook likes any day.

Those same experts are also right when they throw out heady facts, such as: Pinterest delivers more referring website traffic than LinkedIn, YouTube and Tumblr COMBINED...

...and Pinterest users BUY more often than users of other social networks. (And when they do BUY, they spend a hell of a lot more money than Facebookers and Twitterers combined.)

...BUT then there are detractors.

They'll say, "*Pinterest is FINE if you're selling decorative candle holders on Etsy or LuluLemon yoga pants…but if you're not selling a PHYSICAL product, specifically designed for women, then Pinterest offers little more than a way to WASTE valuable marketing resources on a social network that could dissapear in six months.*"

And I have to admit, for the longest time, I was one of those Pinterest naysayers.

For one thing, I'm a GUY.

Spending time on Pinterest feels like being dragged by my wife into Bath and Body Works. I know moisturizing is important. I know scented body washes have their place in this world, but I look around thinking: "This place is…Not. For. Me."

Then I remembered Facebook started out as a whiny social network for Harvard undergrads.

That Twitter was designed as an internal company communication tool that would (hopefully) replace Instant Messaging.

That YouTube was…well…who the hell knows what YouTube was created for.

So, I swallowed my pride, and my inherent distrust of yoga pose photos, and jumped into the swirling vortex of Pinterest.

And, I made EVERY mistake a Pinterest marketer can make. (Most of which I'll show you how to avoid.)

Then, gradually, I started to NOT suck so badly. And what I found was a-stounding.

Pinterest didn't just boost my traffic. It:

☑ Increased my sales

☑ Boosted my email subscriber counts

☑ Reduced product return rates

☑ Cut down on customer support costs

☑ Put me in contact with affiliates and JV partners

☑ Created more leads (and more customers) per dollar spent than Facebook and Twitter

And that's when it occurred to me: Pinterest's appeal isn't just pretty photos collected in a virtual scrapbook.

Pinterest allows people to ORGANIZE their world.

To put their life experience into themed boards that shows their friends — and the rest of the Pinterest universe — who they REALLY are. (Or who they desperately WISH they were.)

Unlike a Facebook page, which has a multitude of voices and rants and complaints (all without any context to one other)…

…or a Twitter feed, which is like drinking from a 140-character social media fire hose…

…or YouTube which is like visiting the cantina from Star Wars. (Who knows what you'll find in there?)

A *Pinterest board*, such as the very popular Nordstrom "Shoe Lust" board with its 156K followers, is about as simple as it gets.

It's about pictures of pretty shoes. That's it.

It's not about users or profiles or friends or retweets or likes or RSS feeds or blog posts or anything that feels like homework…

…it's about a single place where people share pictures of a SPECIFIC thing, such as triathlon exercises, DIY bathroom ideas, Indian curry recipes…whatever.

And having something in our lives that simple, focused, fun, and ultra-visual (meaning we can consume it in a matter of a few seconds) provides real benefit to people living in a crazy, chaotic, smartphone-infused world.

And if, we as marketers, can tell a simple STORY about our products and services, that connect to people on a primal, emotional level…

Then not only will we **sell more stuff,** but we'll be helping our customers connect to that magical, inspirational, kick-ass part of themselves.

And doing that can impact your business, and the world, in ways you can't imagine.

Skeptical?

Think I'm full of Pinterest bull crap? That's okay.

I would have thought I was full of it too.

Until I made money from Pinterest. (Nothing changes one's mind like adding commas to a bank balance.)

So…let's enroll in the department of Pinterest studies and go make you some moo-lah!

Chapter 1:

Pinterest Made Super Simple

"The best way to predict the future is to create it."

-Peter Drucker

Before we jump into the deep end of the Pinterest pool, I want to make sure we're all on the same page. (Nothing more confusing in this world than a social network and all its oddly-named components.)

So, if you feel you got a pretty good handle on what Pinterest is, but you just want to start crushing it from the marketing side, then feel free to jump over to Chapter 2.

But if you're relatively new to Pinterest, and don't know your pinboard from your repin, then up your Pinterest IQ with these answers to these Pinterest FAQs:

PINTEREST FAQ No.1: HOW DO I MAKE MONEY WITH PINTEREST?

How do we turn all these pins and repins and likes and pinboards into hard currency?

Most social networks FROWN on overt selling. (Just see how many times you link out to your sales pages on Facebook before you incur a "fan" revolt.)

But Pinterest is different.

For one thing, the entire Pinterest ecosystem is based on people pinning pictures of:

☑ Stuff They Want

☑ Stuff That Represents Their Style

☑ Stuff That Inspires Them

Market your stuff in a way that touches on one, if not all of those, and you have something that doesn't "feel" like marketing.

Best of all, Pinterest users ARE buyers. They want to spend money on cool stuff. And studies show they spend a ton more than any other social network user. (Nearly double what Facebook and Twitter users spend, combined.)

And if your cool stuff is aligned with their themed pinboards, and the boards of their friends, then you will find a new source of leads who not only share your content and follow your company…but they also **buy your stuff**.

The important thing is you GOTTA tell a story with your product or service. You know, besides, "We sell stuff so we can make money."

Come up with a compelling WHY for your company — "We're an organic diaper company who believes in a no-chemical childhood…" "We're a group of accountants who wear blue jeans and motorcycle jackets to work…" — and you're 75% of the way there with your Pinterest marketing.

PINTEREST FAQ No. 2: YEAH, BUT WHAT IF I DON'T SELL TO WOMEN?

There's no getting around this fact. On Pinterest, every night is ladies' night. (I know they say 65% of all Pinterest users are women, but I think that's being exceedingly generous to the male side.)

But maybe that's not a bad thing.

According to She-Conomy, women represent nearly two-thirds of all consumer spending. (That means whether your product or service is for men OR women, chances are women will end up buying it at some point.)

Now, it should be said, if you're selling something that absolutely no woman would ever want to look at (or even imagine thinking about it) — such as a seduction dating information product or a Hooter's girl calendar — then you may want to think before plunging forward with your Pinterest marketing strategy.

This doesn't mean, though, you can't sell products *designed for men*.

As any advertising expert will tell you: Old Spice's ingenious "The Man Your Man Could Smell Like" ad campaigns were NOT intended for men. (They were designed for my wife. Guess what I'm using for deodorant now.)

PINTEREST FAQ NO.3: WHAT'S A PIN?

A pin is simply an image or video that users add to their Pinterest profile. Somewhat like the Pinterest version of the "tweet" or the Facebook "status update."

That's it. Don't overthink it.

PINTEREST FAQ NO.4: HOW DO I PIN?

There are four different ways to pin something:

- ☑ Clicking the "Pin It" button on a website page.
- ☑ Clicking on your Pinterest bookmarklet in your browser.
- ☑ Adding the website URL in the "Add From a Website" field of your Pinterest dashboard.

☑ Upload an image or video directly to Pinterest.

All pins link back to their original source. (No matter how many times they are shared.)

Pinterest FAQ No.5: What Do I Put Into My Pin?

We're going to cover this in some detail in Chapter 5, but for now just know that when you "pin" something there are three things to consider:

☑ What specific image or video on a web page the pin will feature.

☑ What specific pinboard the pin is associated to.

☑ What's in the text description of the pin. Example: Caption, links, calls-to-action, etc.

Again, this is vital marketer real estate. In Chapter 5, we'll go over the whats and hows of the perfect pin to help you reach your marketing goals.

Pinterest FAQ No.6: Okay, So What's a Pinboard?

Pinboards, or boards, are themed collections of pins. They're kind of like mini-Facebook pages, but without all the Mafia Wars invites.

The whole concept of the pinboard can be a bit confusing the first time out. Just know that:

☑ Each pin is associated to a specific pinboard

☑ You can create as many pinboards as you want

☑ Followers of yours can follow either your entire profile, which means they get updated on everything you do, or they can follow specific, individual boards.

Pinterest FAQ No.7: What Should I Create Pinboards About?

Almost anything you want!

As long as you don't go with what Pinterest gives you out of the box. As a Pinterset user, you are given a few default boards upon signing up. They are called "My Styles" and "Places and Spaces."

These need to be changed immediately. These are horrible names for anything, let alone a Pinterest board.

You can organize a board around almost anything:

☑ A theme

☑ An event

☑ A special promotion

☑ A product or service

☑ Your customers (or a segment of your customers)

☑ Testimonials

☑ Quotes

☑ A special private board that only invited users can contribute to

☑ …anything!

In Chapter 4, I go into a ton more detail on the best practices for creating boards.

Pinterest FAQ No.8: Is a Repin the Same Thing as a Pin

Repins are like retweets. Sorta.

Like retweets, a Pinterest user finds an interesting pin they think is cool. They then repin it to one of their "boards." The original pinner still retains credit for the pin, no matter how many times it is repinned.

Nearly 80% of all the activity on Pinterest is *repins*. They are an important part of your Pinterest strategy, but to separate yourself from the Pinterest pack you'll need to do more pinning than repinning.

Pinterest FAQ No.9: What's a Like? Is it Like a "Facebook Like"?

Yeah, kinda.

When you "like" a specific pin, it is added to your profile's collection of "likes." (I suppose for those folks who feel that the four seconds it takes to "repin" something is more than they're willing to spend.)

"Likes" are not added to a user's particular pinboard, but are instead added to a user's "likes" page. (This is more of a social vote, than a traffic-getting strategy.)

To "like" a pin, simply hover over the pin and "click" on the HEART icon.

Pinterest FAQ No.10: How Do I Make Sure I Don't Waste My Time With Pinterest?

Well, you're reading this book, right? :)

Seriously, there's a minimum-effort threshold I'd like you to think about before crashing the Pinterest marketing party.

Can you or somebody on your team commit to:

☑ Pinning 5-20 pins a day? Remember each of these take about three seconds. (That's almost a full minute's work.)

☑ Following 25-50 other Pinterest users per day?

☑ Creating 10-20 boards for different themes and topics relates to your business? (Just need these to get up and running.)

☑ Throwing an occasional contest to boost your fan base and increase your amount of leads?

☑ Always adding pretty pictures to every piece of web content you produce?

If you can do that, and it seriously shouldn't take you more than 10 minutes a day, you will be light years ahead of 92% of the businesses out there on Pinterest. (And you'll be making a hell of a lot more money than them too.)

Chapter 2:

4 Steps to a Kick-Ass Pinterest Profile

"If you have nothing to create at all, then perhaps you create yourself."

-C.G. Jung

Before we jump into the creation of your fabulous Pinterest boards and start to grow your Pinterest follower base (and make some serious money from our new Pinterest efforts)…

We need to create one seriously kick-ass Pinterest profile.

Because a Pinterest account isn't just where your pins and pinboards live, it's also a huge source of referral website traffic. (And that traffic is especially effective when sent to opt-in pages and sales pages.)

And don't forget your Pinterest profile provides a serious SEO boost to whatever external location it links to. Way bigger than your Facebook or Twitter profiles ever will.

So here are my FOUR Kick-Ass Steps to Creating an Awesome Pinterest Profile to get you primed for domination:

KICK-ASS PINTEREST PROFILE STEP NO.1: CREATE A BUSINESS ACCOUNT

Just like with the Facebook universe, there are two kinds of profiles when it comes to Pinterest: personal and business.

We want the business.

Not just for the obvious reason — that we are, in fact, doing business-y things. But there are some basic, though important, reasons for having a business account:

☑ Promoting your wares on a personal account violates Pinterest's terms of service. (And could get your account banned.)

☑ You can designate your business name as the profile name for a business account. Sounds obvious, but this is not something you can do with a personal account, in which you have to have a regular (first name, surname) naming structure.

☑ As of the writing of this book, Pinterest will be adding some new features for business accounts down the line. (My guess? Cool analytics and more creative profile display options.)

So how do you set up your business account? Here's how:

1. **Go to the dedicated Pinterest business page**. Head over to: http://business.pinterest.com.

2. **Click "Join as a Business."**

3. **Fill out the key info**. Make sure that your company name hasn't already been taken by somebody else. (It happens.)

4. **Add a keyword in the username, if you can**. It's not required: but the username carries a HUGE SEO boost to your profile. (Meaning your Pinterest boards could eventually show up in Google rankings for important keywords.)

5. **Verify your website.**

   Huh? **Verify** your website? What the heck does that mean?

   Well, funny you should ask, because that is…

Kick-Ass Pinterest Profile Step No.2: Verify Your Website

You'd think this would be easy. You'd be wrong.

Pinterest requires all business accounts be "verified" by having the user place code on their website or blog.

Yeah. Code. Sounds fun, doesn't it?

You can do this two different ways:

1. By uploading an HTML file (generated by Pinterest) to your website's server

2. By adding a meta tag (generated by Pinterest) to your website's home page

If what I just said sounds like I'm speaking Klingon, then I'd like to make a recommendation: Head over to a site like Fiverr.com and pay the five bucks to have somebody do it for you. For somebody who knows what they're doing, it'll take five minutes. For us technically-challenged schlubs… who knows?

If you do know your way around FTP and the back-end of your blog, head over to http://punkrockmarketing.com/pinterestverify. There, I've got some detailed instructions on how to do it.

Again, if you're not sure, hire a professional. (Or that precocious 12-year-old cousin of yours who knows everything.)

Kick-Ass Pinterest Profile Step No.3: Create an "About Me" Section That Doesn't Suck

This is where a lot of Pinterest marketers totally screw up.

The "about me" section of your Pinterest profile is valuable real estate. And it shouldn't be wasted on some rambling pointless dissertation of what kind of DIY bathroom project you're into or your favorite kind of homemade incense.

In the "About Me" section you can:

- ☑ **Talk about the benefits** of your company's products or services. Remember: People care about benefits, not features.

- ☑ **Add in appropriate keywords**. If you're not sure which keywords are the best, head over to http://punkrockmarketing.com/keywordtool. I've got a step-by-step process on a FREE resource to help you out.

- ☑ **If you're a local business, PLEASE use some geo-targeted keywords** in this section. Not abbreviations; good, old spelled-out cities.

- ☑ **Link to your Twitter account**. If you have one that you update frequently.

- ☑ **Link to a landing page other than your home page**. Such as a place to collect email addresses. (You are collecting email addresses, right?)

Kick-Ass Pinterest Profile Step No.4: One Killer Profile Image to Rule Them All

You wouldn't think this would make a difference.

You'd be wrong.

Pinterest is all about pictures, and nowhere is that more evident than with your Pinterest profile image.

Here's what you need to know about profile images:

1. **The image should be a square.** Pinterest recommends an upload size of 600 pixels by 600 pixels to allow for the highest amount of resolution. (And if that's what they recommend, that's probably what we should do.)

2. **The image should focus on one subject.** The picture will be resized to 165 pixels by 165 pixels and group shots can look muddled at that size. (So can vague, indeterminate nature shots.)

3. **People shots are best, if they are crisp.** No blurry, fuzzy iPhone shots you took in the dark holding a margarita.

4. **The image should evoke a "feeling" that relates somehow to your company.** This can be loosely defined, but go for whatever positive feeling you'd like associated with your product and website. (Whether it's a rainbow...or your CEO. Or your CEO standing in front of a rainbow!)

5. **Avoid logos, unless they're awesome.** I don't personally like logos used as profile images. (Think they come off as too artificial.) But if you got a killer one, then feel free to use it.

6. **The name of the image should contain your company name.** Not "IMG_1" or "Pinterest_Logo," but instead "ABC-Accounting" or "Joe's-Pool-Cleaning." This will give your Pinterest account some extra SEO juice.

CHAPTER 2 Key Takeaways:

☑ Create a Pinterest business account. (It'll make your life much easier.)

☑ Verify your website. If you're a bit tech-y, you can upload an HTML file or meta tag to your website. If not, hire somebody to do it for you.

☑ Fill up the "about me" section of your profile with goodies. Add keywords, links and benefits of your business in this valuable part of your profile.

☑ Find a great profile image that is: 600x600 pixels, features one subject, shows people (or a great logo) and has your company name in the file name.

Chapter 3:

7 Tools Every Pinterest Marketer Must Have

"If all you have is a hammer in the toolbox, everything looks like a nail."

-Bernard Baruch

Okay, here's where we separate from the pack.

Here's where we stand out from the rest of the Pinterest hobbyists and flex some serious Pinterest marketing muscle.

Most of the tools I advocate below are 100% FREE. (And my favorite tool costs less than a couple of bucks a month.)

No joke…adding these tools to your Pinterest marketing arsenal will make it MUCH EASIER to attract leads and find those elusive, paying customers.

So, here are my SEVEN Must-Have Pinterest Tools to get you ready for maximum Pinterest marketing supremacy:

Must-Have Pinterest Tool No.1: A Camera That Doesn't Royally Suck

Nothing sells a product on Pinterest like a kick-ass photo. And chances are you already have a decent well-stocked camera sitting in your pocket.

That's right. Your smartphone!

Most smartphones made in the last couple of years pack plenty of camera-taking punch to suit your needs. (If you know how to use it right.)

Here are a few quick tips when taking photos with your smartphone:

☑ **Turn the phone sideways.** This gives you more photo-editing area to work with later. Nothing screams "amateur" like a vertical smartphone photo.

☑ **Tap on the screen to indicate the subject of the picture.** This lets the phone do all kinds of auto-focus and stabilization stuff that'll make your photo sing.

☑ **Lean against a wall or some kind of flat surface.** This avoids needless movement which can affect crispness and photo clarity.

And what do ya do if you don't have a smartphone?

Well, for just a couple hundred dollars you could buy something from the very under-rated and high-performing Canon PowerShot series. (You could, of course, spend a lot more on a Digital SLR camera. But if that's the case, you certainly don't need my camera-buying tips.)

No matter what your camera of choice, here are a couple of general tips when shooting people or products:

☑ **Shoot outside if you can.** Natural light is always better than artificial light.

☑ **Late mornings (8:30 a.m. - 10:00 a.m.) and late afternoons (4:00 p.m. - 6:00 p.m.) are "magic" times** to shoot photos because the lighting is warm. Noontime is the worst, it makes people look like vampires.

☑ **"Don't look into the light!"** Always try to shoot with the sun to your back.

☑ **Keep it even.** If shooting inside, try to keep the light source behind you consistent on all sides. (You can buy desk lamps and clip them behind you, if needed.)

MUST-HAVE PINTEREST TOOL NO. 2: FREE (AND LEGAL) SOURCES FOR PHOTOS

Not all the images you share on Pinterest are gonna be ones that came from your camera. (For one thing, nobody wants to look at your product pics all day. Secondly, you gotta a frickin' business to run.)

That's why it's crucial to find sources for FREE (and legal) photos you can use under the Creative Commons license. **Note:** Creative Commons has a wide variety of rights distinctions. It's worth learning about. Just head over to: http://en.wikipedia.org/wiki/Creative_Commons to get more information about it.

The LEGAL part of "Legal and Free" is important. You don't want to just grab pics from Google Images. It's wrong, and could get you thrown into a Bulgarian work camp.

Here are some of my favorite places to grab open-source photos: (Note: Be sure to check the copyright on all images before using)

☑ PhotoBin (http://photobin.com)

☑ Flickr (http://flickr.com)

☑ Morgue File (http://morguefile.com)

☑ Stock Exchange (http://www.sxc.hu/)

And when you're on the look-out for photos remember:

☑ **You gotta GRAB people**. You want crisp, sharp photos... that stand out! Better to be shocking than boring.

☑ **Forget pretty, go with real**. Stock photos of supermodels doing "ordinary" things look staged and really DUMB.

☑ **Go with your gut.** Find photos that evoke a "feeling," don't just look for photos that make literal sense.

Must-Have Pinterest Tool No.3: PicMonkey

The really cool thing about photo-editing tools, such as the supremely awesome PicMonkey (http://punkrockmarketing. com/monkey), is it makes you look like a much better photographer than you actually are. (As a very mediocre photographer myself, this is a great asset.)

Now, you don't HAVE to use PicMonkey. You could use FREE tools such as Gimp, or really expensive tools like Photoshop.

But PicMonkey is my secret Pinterest marketing weapon because it's:

☑ Cheap — they have a FREE option and a very reasonable paid option.

☑ Easy to Use.

☑ Very Powerful — lets you correct lighting issues and offers a TON of out-of-the-box effects that are perfect for making your photos POP.

☑ Made for non-techie folks (like me).

☑ Lets you add a company watermark to your images

But I think the BIGGEST benefit PicMonkey gives you is the ability to add a text overlay to your photos.

This is HUGE. With a text overlay you can:

☑ Add quotes to images. Wanna create a viral meme? Just put a quote over a pretty picture.

☑ Ask people to visit your website.

☑ Ask people to "pin" a photo.

☑ Suggest people sign up for your email list to get a free thing you're giving away.

And the crazy thing is: just asking people to "pin" your photo increases engagement by 80%.

I know. It shouldn't be that easy. Telling people you want them to do something...then having them do it.

But it can be! And PicMonkey is in, my never humble opinion, the best friend a Pinterest marketer can have.

MUST-HAVE PINTEREST TOOL No.4: PICTURES (AND LOTS OF 'EM) ON YOUR WEBSITE

This one isn't so much a tool as it is a best practice.

If you aren't already adding a picture to every piece of content you publish on your site — whether it be a blog post, essay, FAQ, About page, deranged manifesto about the government, etc. — then you are missing out on a huge source of Pinterest traffic.

We've touched briefly on what KIND of photos to look for. (Crisp, interesting, no supermodels using laundry detergent.) But here's what you need to know before uploading actual photos to your site:

☑ **"Name" the photo with a keyword**. For instance, if the blog post is about "How to Make Decorative Candles," then a great picture name would be: "Decorative_Candles," not "Photo1."

☑ **Get in fast**. Try to get the photo in the first couple paragraphs of your blog post or webpage.

☑ Caption this! If you have room for a caption, be sure to include a keyword there as well.

Must-Have Pinterest Tool No.5: Pinterest Buttons...Everywhere!

Pinterest buttons let you leverage the existing website and blog traffic you are already getting to your site and encourages those visitors to pin your existing content. (Now you know WHY it's so important to make sure all your groovy content is adorned with killer images.)

Creating the button is really simple; it's just a matter of generating some code you throw onto your site.

To do this, head over to http://punkrockmarketing.com/pinterestbutton to generate the code. You'll find a couple of design and text options. Nothing fancy, but it'll get the job done.

There are two important types of buttons to focus on:

a.   **The Pin It Button:** This lets folks pin a photo located on a specific web page to the pin board of their choosing.

b.   **The "Follow" Button:** This lets people "follow" you on Pinterest.

So where do we put these buttons? Here's how I use the "Pin It Button":

☑   In the body of a blog post

☑   The sidebar of a website

☑   The header of a website

☑   The footer of every blog post

☑   Next to every video

And as for the "Follow on Pinterest" button, I make sure it can be found in places like:

☑   The "Thank You for Subscribing" page

☑   The checkout page

☑ The email signature

☑ The message board profile signatures

☑ The website footer

MUST-HAVE PINTEREST TOOL NO.6: GET A PINTEREST BOOKMARKLET

I know. I hate the term bookmarklet too. (Offends my English-Major sensibilities.) But they're huge Pinterest time-savers.

Basically a "bookmarklet" is an extension you install on your web browser of choice that lets you "pin" things to your Pinterest profile with the simple click of a button. (Told ya Pinterest takes way less time than other social networks.)

To set up the bookmarklet, just head over to http://about.pinterest.com/goodies/ and you can grab the bookmarklet thing-y. (You can even get the Pinterest smartphone app there as well.)

MUST-HAVE PINTEREST TOOL NO.7: PUT A BOARD WIDGET ON YOUR WEBSITE

Before you say: "What the hell is a board widget? And why should I care?…"

…a board widget is simply a piece of code you throw onto your website that shows your website visitors the latest pins from your Pinterest account. (Another good reason to separate the personal from the business with your Pinterest activities.)

Now, in the early days of your Pinterest career, this widget will look skimpy. But before you know it, you'll have a robust Pinterest offering. (And what better way to show off your Pinterest efforts and "spice" up your website, visually, than adding a little board widget action?)

To generate the code, just head over to that same location I mentioned earlier (http://punkrockmarketing.com/pinterest-button) to get your board widget created and your website looking somewhat less sucky.

CHAPTER 3 KEY TAKEAWAYS:

☑ Make sure you have a halfway decent camera. You don't need a full-on DSLR; your smartphone will most likely work.

☑ Shoot outside, if possible. Always keep the camera steady, with the light to your back.

☑ Great places to find free (legal) photos are PhotoBin, MorgueFile and Flickr. (Be sure to check on the rights of every photo you use.)

☑ Get awesome photos with PicMonkey. Be sure to add text overlays that encourage folks to "pin" your photos.

☑ Go photo crazy. Include a crisp, interesting photo with every piece of content you publish on your site.

☑ Add Pinterest buttons — both "Pin It" buttons and "Follow Me" buttons — everywhere on your site. That includes headers, footers, sidebars, thank you pages and in the body of all your content.

☑ Grab the Pinterest bookmarklet to save you a bunch of time.

☑ Place a board widget on your site, especially if your site needs a bit of sprucing up.

Chapter 4:

The Marvelous & Fantastic World of PinBoards

"Great works are performed not by strength but by perseverance."

-Samuel Johnson

This chapter will blow your mind.

Seriously, when you discover some of the cool, awesome things you can do with Pinboards you might just need hospitalization from your instant Pinterest awesomeness.

While it's true most casual users experience Pinterest through the pins they use to tag whatever catches their eye, it's really the BOARDS that give us HUGE marketing potential.

Because Pinterest boards are like little silos of super-focused, ultra-targeted awesomeness that let users check out our products, share our content and eventually buy our stuff.

As I said earlier, unlike its social-media cohort, Facebook, a Pinterest user does not follow EVERY single thing you do on Pinterest.

That means users can just "follow" and check out the things they want. Example: A user can "follow" a Nordstrom board dedicated to Prada shoes, without having to follow the "Coach handbag" board, which they may or may not have any interest in.

And, most importantly, it means you can meet your prospective customers in a huge variety of ways. (And sell them a huge variety of products and services.)

So, now you've got the 411 of how Pinterest boards actually work, let's show you how to plan, create and fill those boards with awesome money-making content.

And we'll do that with my little THREE-Step Blueprint to a Kick-Ass Pinterest Board:

KICK-ASS BLUEPRINT STEP NO.1: REALIZE WHAT'S POSSIBLE

I used to think Pinterest boards were just a place to house all my product photos and affiliate crap.

Boy, was I wrong.

There is (virtually) no limit to the things you can do with Pinterest boards. There are a couple of obvious options:

☑ Create a board for each different product or service you offer in your business.

☑ Create a board where customers can give you feedback on your products.

☑ Create a board where customers can find out about any big company news or future product launches.

And, yeah, that's nice. But it doesn't EVEN scratch the surface. Here's some other really cool board ideas:

☑ A testimonial board for your products, where followers and customers can leave comments.

☑ A board highlighting members of your company. (People LOVE these.)

☑ A board showing behind-the-scenes stuff about your company. Videos work great here.

☑ A board promoting and recapping a live event.

☑ A board that offers how-to advice on a specific topic. (Lowe's does a great job of this with their DIY boards.)

☑ A board that offers supplemental training. (This can work great for info-product creators and those in the education-al space.)

☑ A board that spotlights some of your top clients or cus-tomers. (You can imagine the goodwill this might create.)

☑ A board specifically for affiliates.

☑ A board for any special offer, coupon, contest, promotion, or product.

The possibilities are endless. If you've got some rich media (photos, video, audio) that can be themed and organized... then putting them into a board is a great idea.

KICK-ASS BLUEPRINT STEP NO.2: COME UP WITH A BOARD PLAN

So now you've got some ideas of the kind of boards you COULD create, it's time to brainstorm all of the different kinds of boards you SHOULD make.

Not all of the boards I mentioned earlier will be relevant to your business. And that's okay.

What you want to do is think outside the box. Come up with interesting, creative ways you can show off your company and its offerings.

Here are a couple of questions to get you and your team started:

☑ How many different products and services does my busi-ness have?

☑ Do we have happy customers/clients we'd like to spotlight?

☑ Are there certain areas of expertise where we could be a resource to potential customers?

☑ What would be the best way to break up these areas of expertise into separate boards? (Again, Lowe's does this really well: breaking up the DIY boards by project.)

☑ Do we have upcoming events that would make for cool boards? (If so, make damn sure SOMEBODY takes a lot of photos and video.)

☑ Do we have any future product launches or new services that could use a board?

☑ What would be a really cool, interesting way to feature our team? (Videos? Blog posts? Pictures of our employees' pets?)

Try to shoot for at least 10 or so boards that can have at least 25-50 pins apiece. This will be enough to get you started, and help your Pinterest account look thriving and robust.

Kick-Ass Blueprint Step No.3: Create Your Boards (and Give 'Em Non-Sucky Names)

Okay, so now you got a plan! It's time to dig in and create your boards.

The HOW is pretty simple. You just:

☑ Click the Add+ button in the upper right-hand corner of your Pinterest home page.

☑ Select the "Create a Board" option.

☑ Enter the name, category, and (any) contributors to the board…then click "Create Board."

But there's a couple important things to keep in mind when creating your boards:

- ☑ **Try to get a keyword in if you can.** Your SEO ranking will thank you for it.

- ☑ **Put a twist at the end to give your board name a bit of personality.** Instead of "Marketing Tips," you could do: a) "Marketing Tips From Andy" or "Marketing Tips From the Lab" or the very simple "Marketing Tips That Don't Suck."

- ☑ **You CAN change the name of your board later.** BUT changing the name changes the URL. So if you have links to that particular board, it may break those links.

- ☑ **Don't stress the "category" choice too much.** Pinterest doesn't give you a lot of options. And most of the ones they do give you are boring.

- ☑ **Add contributors, if relevant.** Pinterest boards can create some seriously cool micro-communities. So if it's part of the board plan, specify here who can contribute to your board.

CHAPTER 4 KEY TAKEAWAYS:

☑ There are TONS of different ways you can theme and organize your Pinterest boards. My personal favorites include: 1) Highlighting customers 2) Collecting testimonials 3) Employee spotlights 4) How-to resources 5) Affiliate boards and 6) Future product launches.

☑ Brainstorm different boards that might work for your business. Anything that tells a "story" with pictures and video would work.

☑ Be sure to include keywords in your board names. And add a bit of "spice" at the end to stand out from the pack.

Chapter 5:

4 Keys to the Perfect Pin

"Bite off more than you can chew, then chew it."

-Courage Wolf

Ah, yes. Pins.

The raw currency that makes the Pinterest economy go.

Pins aren't QUITE like Facebook status updates and tweets. For one thing they last forever. (As opposed to tweets and Facebook updates, which can be edited and deleted.)

And pins aren't simply a "vote" for something a user likes. Such as a Facebook "like" or "retweet."

When somebody "pins" a photo, they decide which "board" that "pin" will live in. And that "pin" becomes a part of their board ecosystem, not just something to fill their newsfeed.

So, offering compelling and interesting content that people will "pin" and "repin" is our primary job as Pinterest marketing gurus. Filling our boards with pin-worthy goodies is an important first step to attracting followers and building up our Pinterest street cred.

So, that's what we're going to do.

In this chapter I'm going to show you my FOUR Keys to the Perfect Pin:

Note: If you don't quite remember your pins from your repins — and honestly, why should you? — head over to Chapter 1, where I go over that in some detail.

How Pinning Works

Here's a super-brief primer on how to "pin" something:

1. **You decide on something to pin.** Either through uploading a photo or video, using your bookmarklet browser extension, clicking on a web location's "pin it" button or pasting the URL directly into your Pinterest dashboard.

2. You choose **which of your boards** the pin will live in.

3. **Fill out the pin's description**…and you're done!

How Repinning Works

This is even more simple. You find a "pin" somebody else has already shared on Pinterest and:

1. Hover over the pin and click "Pin It"

2. Select which board you want to add the repin to

3. Click "Pin It"

As my 15-year-old emo cousin would say: "It ain't rocket surgery."

What You Should Fill Your Boards With

This is really the big question facing us as marketers. How much NEW, original pinning do we do?

And how much repinning (or using other people's content) should we do? Especially since repinning is a great way to grab new followers. (More on that in the next chapter.)

If it's a board focused on internal/company stuff — such as an "employee spotlight" board or a "client appreciation" board — then obviously the pins associated with that board will be limited in scope. And repinning will play less of a role.

Although, when appropriate, opening up the board to outside contributors can lead to some interesting content you hadn't thought of being shared on the board.

But if it's a board that is about a more general theme or area of expertise — such as a "DIY Bathroom Project" board — I like to keep the mix of pins somewhere in the neighborhood of:

☑ 25% repins

☑ 25% pins of other resources (Such as blog posts, YouTube videos, anything I didn't create)

☑ 50% featuring my own company's blog posts, images, videos, and photos.

Now you may NOT have enough visual content to fill up that 50%. And that's okay. Do what you can.

Just commit you and your team to creating more visual content — could be as simple as putting an inspirational quote on a pretty picture — from here on out.

Alright, enough of the jibber-jabber…let's get to the 4 Keys to the Perfect Pin!

PERFECT PIN KEY NO.1: FIND COOL STUFF TO PIN

This will, of course, depend on the specific board you are pinning items to, but here's the stuff that's worked best for me:

☑ **Inspirational quotes over pretty pictures.** (This NEVER fails.)

☑ **Product stills.** Make sure they are crisp and non-sucky.

☑ **Photos and videos of my team** doing human, non salesey things.

☑ **How-to videos.** Both that we created and curated from somewhere else.

☑ **Infographics**. If you want some resources on how to create your own totally FREE infographic, check out http://punkrockmarketing.com/infographic.

☑ **Funny videos and pictures**. If you can get an animal in there, even better.

☑ **Checklists, insider guides, cheat sheets**. Anything that smells like a resource.

☑ **Repins of other Pinterest users** that fit in with the theme of your board.

And where do you find all of these assets?

Well here are some of my favorite go-to spots:

☑ **PopUrls:** (http://popurls.com) This "best of" collection of the stuff that's viral and popular on the Internet is my browser home page. (You'll find a broad range of content here, from the slightly profane to the scholarly erudite.) Poke around and you might just find the perfect stuff to add to your Pinterest stew.

☑ **AllTop: (**http://alltop.com) This is a site that collects the best blog posts on the web about a given topic. And it's done by humans! Check it out, there's virtually a page about everything here.

☑ **Photo of the Day:** There are tons of Photo of the Day (Google "photo of the day") sites. Pick one that fits your business and use it to fill up your Pinterest archive.

☑ **Google Alerts:** (http://google.com/alerts) This tool allows you to set up alerts, based on keywords, that will have ALL of the latest blog posts, news stories, discussions, etc., about that topic delivered to your inbox.

I like to create a Google Doc where my team and I can throw in URLs for interesting visual stuff we come across in the course of our workday. (You'll be shocked how quickly your Pinterest reserves can fill up.)

The key thing is to mix it up. Don't pin everything you see from The New York Times and The Daily Beast. Keep it varied.

Step No.2: Decide on the Best Time to Pin

This is not written in stone. But according to Reachli, a Pinterest analytics company, the best times to post on Pinterest are between 2:00 p.m. - 4:00 p.m. EST and again from 8:00 p.m. - 1:00 a.m. EST.

And I have to agree.

Pinterest is definitely an afternoon, after-work activity. So play around with your posting times, but late afternoon and evening definitely seem to work best. If you're a local business, start with evenings and work backwards to find your pinning sweet spot.

Step No.3: Write a Great Pin Description (and Tell People What You Want Them to Do)

It's in the description of your pin where the juicy marketing stuff happens.

There are four key things to include in every pin description you write:

1. **Keywords in the body of the text.** But not in an overdone, spammy sort of way. This will help people find your pins and boards in both the Pinterest search engine and external website search engines.

2. **A call-to-action** that tells people to either find out more about your product or service, opt-in to your email list or buy your product or service outright.

3. **An external link** for people to follow, based on the call-to-action you give them. Don't put in a shortened URL, such as http://bitly/375. These tend to be seen as spam. Put the entire link, including "http," in the description.

4. **(Optional) The price of the product featured in the pin description.** This is done by simply typing the $ or £ in your description and adding the amount. (Pinterest will automatically add the price in a text overlay on the photo. Pretty cool, huh?)

Some Pinterest gurus recommend you add #hashtags to your Pinterest description. You know, to help your pins get easily located in the Pinterest archives.

I don't advise this.

Adding a hashtag in your description simply gives people an invitation to leave your pin and check out a bunch of other people's stuff. (Pinterest users have a short enough attention span. I don't need to help it along any with some needless hashtags.)

STEP No.4: SHARE YOUR PIN ON FACEBOOK AND TWITTER

You do have a Facebook Page and Twitter account? Right?

Well, Pinterest makes it super simple to have your pins automatically show up as updates and tweets in your other social media platforms.

All you do is:

- ☑ Look under Pinterest settings
- ☑ Click on "Social Networks"
- ☑ Choose which social network you'd like Pinterest to share your activity with.

And yet, I'd like you to tread carefully with this.

The Twitter integration is fine, I ain't too worried about that. Twitter moves so fast, and there's so much stuff out there, that it's hardly worth worrying about.

But, with Facebook, it's very possible to overload your fans. Studies have shown posting more than twice a day on a Facebook page actually suppresses engagement.

So instead, I recommend you simply add a Pinterest tab to your Facebook page. That way if people want to check out your "pins" they can do so there, but they won't feel overloaded with content.

To install the Pinterest app on your Facebook page, simply install the totally FREE WooBox Pinterest app. (http://woobox.com/pinterest)

All you gotta do is:

- ☑ Head over to WooBox.com
- ☑ Click "Get Started for Free"
- ☑ Sync the app up with your Facebook Page (You'll need to be signed up to do this)

...and you're done! Su-per easy. (And it makes your Facebook page look a lot more filled out as well.)

CHAPTER 5   KEY TAKEAWAYS:

☑ Pinning success starts with finding great content to share. (PopUrls, AllTop, Google Alerts and Photo-of-the-Day sites are perfect for this.)

☑ Keep it visual. Other good pieces of content to pin include: infographics, how-to stuff, product stills that don't suck, quote overlays on photos, and behind-the-scenes content.

☑ Watch the clock. The best time to pin SEEMS to be late afternoon, and after dinner. (Test to find the best time for you.)

☑ Use the description wisely. Include keywords, price points, and external links to your site in the description.

☑ Promote your pins on Twitter and Facebook. Set up the Twitter integration within the Pinterest dashboard, but create a Pinterest custom tab on your Facebook page to avoid fatiguing your Facebook fans.

Chapter 6:

7 Killer Strategies for Getting More Followers

"Why join the Navy if you can be a pirate?"

-Steve Jobs

All the pins and pinboards in the world won't do you much good if you don't have followers.

And that's what we're going to cover in this chapter: the subtle (and not-so-subtle) art of attracting Pinterest followers. (Who we can eventually turn into customers.)

In the next chapter I'm going to show you how to actually make some money from your Pinterest tribe. But for now, we gotta build the tribe before we can ask it to do things. (Like buy stuff from us!)

So, here are my SEVEN Top Tips for Finding a Collection of Rabid, Passionate (and Wallet-Opening) Pinterest Followers:

RABID FOLLOWER TIP NO.1: PIN MORE STUFF

What? You mean I gotta pin…like…more stuff?

'Fraid so.

Pinterest rewards the dedicated, and slightly obsessed, with a ton of new followers. But those followers are like four-year-olds in a Chuck E. Cheese restaurant.

Easily. Distracted.

That's why you got to keep the flow of pins, and pepperoni pizza, coming.

Research shows that the ideal pin sweet spot seems to be around 4-25 times a day. Which sounds like a lot. (I know.)

Until you realize it takes all of four seconds to pin something. (And if you've got the Pinterest bookmarklet added to your browser, less than that.)

The key thing is to come up with some kind of pinning routine that everybody on your team can follow.

This is the schedule I follow:

☑ 9:30 a.m. - Coffee Break: Three pins

☑ Noon - Lunchtime: Three repins

☑ 3:30 p.m. - Afternoon break: Three pins

☑ 7:00 p.m. - Evening pin session: Three repins

☑ 10:00 p.m. - Late-evening pin session: Three pins

Seriously, this takes me less than 10 minutes total. Each day.

And by following this system I get myself 15 pins a day. Have other people on your team pitch in and before you know it your Pinterest pin total will be through the roof.

RABID FOLLOWER TIP No.2: REPIN FOLKS

This works the same as it does with Twitter. (Even more so.)

The fact is: after you repin somebody, they are VERY likely to follow you back. (Most people are still REALLY NEW to Pinterest and having some kind of social interaction with people is pretty cool.)

To keep it simple, I dedicate specific blocks of my pinning time to repinning. As my aforementioned schedule revealed, I focus my lunchtime and after-dinner pinning sessions to repinning. (Which is good, because after I eat, all my brain cells can pretty much handle is repinning.)

This does a couple of cool things.

If somebody is on their lunch break, and gets a smartphone notification that I repinned them, they're **pretty likely** to follow me.

And for the after-dinner session, early evening is prime Pinterest time, so I've got a great chance of adding that user to my tribe while they're in the midst of some serious Pinterest activity.

But experiment. Find out what works for you.

Just make sure you devote SOME time to repinning. (Your bank account will thank you.)

RABID FOLLOWER TIP No.3: FOLLOW YOUR IDEAL CUSTOMERS

This tip requires a bit of detective work. (And a bit of manual labor.)

But you want to put yourself in the mind of your ideal customer by asking:

- ☑ What type of boards would my ideal customer follow?
- ☑ What keywords or phrases would they type into Pinterest?
- ☑ What are they looking for? (If your product or service fills a need or solves a problem, how would they find you?)

And then it's as simple as:

1. Type a keyword related to your ideal customer in the Pinterest search bar.

2. Choose the "Pinners" tab.

3. Start following "pinners" who share "pins" related to that keyword.

4. Follow approximately 50-100 people per "following" session.

5. Give 'em three days to follow you back. If they don't, unfollow them.

6. Rinse and repeat three times a week.

This is the same process I use to build my various Twitter tribes into the tens of thousands.

It's slow. It's monotonous. And it totally works.

Rabid Follower Tip No. 4: Follow the RIGHT Boards

This is exactly the same process as following "pinners." Only after you put your keyword in the Pinterest search bar, you choose "boards" instead of "pinners."

Give the creator of the board a couple of days to follow you back. If not, unfollow them. (Same as the pinner strategy: I like to do this three times a week, shooting for 20-30 new boards to follow each time.)

Rabid Follower Tip No.5: Comment on Popular Pins

This is a super easy technique that a lot of Pinterest marketers neglect. All you do is:

☑ Head over to http://pinterest.com/popular.

☑ Find a couple of cool images that genuinely move you.

☑ Make a comment that doesn't suck.

You don't want to just say: "Agree" or "That's great."

Take your time. Look at the image.

Read the description and make a halfway decent, meaningful comment. People love recognition, especially when it's sincere and heartfelt.

If you're absolutely stumped, just show you're passionate for the subject. (Even if you aren't.)

RABID FOLLOWER TIP No.6: FIND YOUR FRIENDS

This only works if you have actual, human friends. If you're a hermit living in a cave in eastern Mongolia, this won't help.

Once you've connected your other social networks to your Pinterest account — we went over this in Chapter 5 — you can easily look for those same friends and fans on Pinterest.

All you gotta do is:

1. Click on the name of your business account in the upper right-hand corner
2. Select "Find Friends"
3. Follow those "friends"
4. Wait for your Pinterest follower numbers to skyrocket

RABID FOLLOWER TIP No.7:
RUN A CONTEST

Pinterest and contests go together like Lennon and McCartney. Simon and Garfunkel. Lady Gaga and...whatever weird outfit she's wearing these days.

Pinterest users LOVE contests. And they are a fan-tastic way to build your follower base REALLY fast.

Which is why we're devoting an entire chapter to Pinterest contests in Chapter 8. (They're that awesome!)

CHAPTER 6 KEY TAKEAWAYS:

☑ Pin to win. The more you pin, the more followers you'll get.

☑ Repin to find followers. People love recognition, and if you repin them they are likely to follow you back.

☑ Find your ideal customer. Use keywords in the Pinterest search bar and search for "pinners" who are pinning about areas related to your business.

☑ Follow related boards. Use the same "search" feature to find Pinterest boards that might contain folks who would make great followers for your account.

☑ Hang with the popular kids. Head over to pinterest.com/popular and comment on popular pins that are zooming up the Pinterest charts.

☑ Find your friends (if you have some). Use your Pinterest dashboard to connect with your existing social circle to broaden your Pinterest fan base.

Chapter 7:

7 Super Ninja Ways to Make Money With Pinterest

"Nothing makes a man so adventerous as an empty pocket."

-Victor Hugo

Okay, we've gone over some of the more traditional ways to incorporate Pinterest into your marketing arsenal. Create some boards, pin some stuff, sell your wares, buy yourself a yacht...

But there are some real out-of-the-box ways you can use Pinterest to kick-ass marketing effect.

And, trust me, your competition isn't doing any of these.

So, here are my SEVEN Super Ninja Ways to Use Pinterest That Nobody Knows About:

SUPER-NINJA PINTEREST TIP NO. 1: USE PINTEREST AS SOCIAL PROOF

Social proof is just a fancy phrase for using other people's positive opinions about a product or service to help future customers buy more of your stuff.

And it works really well.

If you've got an array of products for sale on your website, why not put a little button next to the products that are most popular on Pinterest? (The fact that your organic eco-friendly baby diapers got 345 pins may not mean that much to you, but it means something to your customers.)

As consumers, we are always trying to compare and judge things in our brain. That's why Amazon reviews and Consumer Reports ratings are so important. So make that job easier for your customers by putting a product's Pinterest popularity front and center.

Note: This works even better with a brick-and-mortar store where shop owners can put ACTUAL Pinterest stickers on price tags.

Super-Ninja Pinterest Tip No.2: Have Customers Vote

The only thing people love more than sharing their opinion, is sharing that opinion when it counts for something.

One technique that works really well is to display two products on your store's showroom floor, or show pictures of two products on a dedicated website landing page, and have customers "vote" on their favorite, with the "winning" item being put on sale for some period of time. Talk about consumer power.

Of course, later on you can feature the winner in your store or on your website as a Pinterest bestseller. (You could even do a press release around the winner, with background on how you ran the contest. Journalists love behind-the-scenes stuff like that.)

And all of that interaction with your Pinterest account makes it much more likely customers will become Pinterest followers (And, hopefully, long-term customers.)

Super-Ninja Pinterest Tip No.3: Create a Product Bundle Board

Folks love getting a deal. And there's nothing that feels quite like a killer deal than a product bundle.

If you've got a suite of products or services, then why not create a board that shows off these assets and offers a bundled price as well? (Say, if you were a flower company offering "wedding flower packages.")

All you do is set up a board with all your relevant products, and link each of the pins' descriptions to a landing page with a discounted bundle price. (And don't forget to promote this themed bundle on all your other social media platforms. A press release wouldn't hurt either.)

Super-Ninja Pinterest Tip No.4: Create a Client-Specific Board

Earlier we talked about creating a board that specifically recognizes a special client or board. But this tip takes that strategy much further.

What if you were a wedding planner? Would creating a client-specific board be a good idea?

Hell yeah!

Or what if you were a realtor? Would creating a client-specific board showing them photos of possible houses be a cool way to give them housing options?

I'd say so!

This may not be practical for everybody, especially those who sell low-ticket items. But if you deal in any kind of sizeable margin items with your business, this would be a great way to offer your clients and customers a fantastic visual way to have their needs met.

Super Ninja Pinterest Tip No.5: Run the Cheapest Focus Group Ever

Would knowing what your ideal customer wants, fears, and secretly desires be helpful to selling more stuff?

Uhh..yeah!

Well, skip the $500 per hour consultant and run your very own focus group.

Simply check out the boards of your followers and find out:

☑ What their passions are

☑ What super expensive merchandise they dream about owning

☑ What they want to look like

☑ What they feel is lacking in their life

☑ What kind of life they dream of having

And then collect all that data into a spreadsheet. (Interns, and teenage children, are perfect for this type of task.)

Once you have your data, brainstorm new products and services that solve these problems and connect with your customers on a deep and personal level. (Where all the real selling takes place.)

Super Ninja Pinterest Tip No.6: Do What You Do Best

My grandfather had an expression: "Feed the stallions and starve the ponies."

And while my Grandad may not have been a fan of the SPCA, the truth is he was right: you gotta exploit what's working and minimize what's not.

Nowhere is that more true than in your inbound marketing. And there's no better way to find what's working — and what's not — on your website then to discover which content from your website people are pinning.

To find this out, all you have to do is add your website into the following path:

Http://pinterest.com/source/yourwebsiteurl.com/ (Just to be crystal clear: you replace "yourwebsiteurl" with your own website. Don't want you wandering off into some weird corner of the Internet.)

This will give you a visual look at what's catching people's eyes. (And what's just sitting there like a mouse fart.)

Bonus: you might even come up with a couple of cool product ideas based on the content people are responding to.

Super Ninja Pinterest Tip No.7: Show Off Your Team (and Your Expertise)

As any overpriced marketing guru will tell you, we buy from people we like.

Ever been to a bookstore and suddenly you come across that "Staff Picks" section? You know the part of the store where over-qualified English majors share their literary faves?

Suddenly you find yourself buying that depressing novel about Seattle oyster farmers in the 1890s because "Katie" the cashier said it "changed her life" and helped her appreciate the "moody, turbulence" of the Pacific Northwest.

Without you realizing it, they've put a human face to their brick-and-mortar business and made you feel "connected." (And sold you crap you didn't want in the first place.)

So what better way to up the "like" quotient of your team than create a dedicated Team Pin Board where your staff can share:

☑ Cool things that inspire them

☑ Recent company outings

☑ The latest visually creative stuff they're working on

☑ Possible creative choices that followers could vote on (People love to feel included)

And you can also use this Pinterest real estate to:

☑ Call out a team member's recent accomplishment

☑ Brainstorm ideas for future products

☑ Share company logos (old and new)

CHAPTER 7 KEY TAKEAWAYS:

☑ Use testimonials. Create a dedicated board where your customers and fans can gush about your products and services.

☑ Let them vote. Pit two of your products against each other to see what the Pinterest community likes best. (Be sure the winner goes on discount after the contest.)

☑ Create a bundle board. Organize your products and services into bundles that you can place on a board and offer at a discounted group price.

☑ Recognize your special clients. Create a dedicated board for your best customers. (They'll love you for it.)

☑ Run a focus group. Do some product research by poking around your ideal customers' boards and pins.

☑ Find out what's working. Check out what people are pinning from your site to discover the effectiveness of your content and potential product ideas.

☑ Show off, but in a nice way. Create a board that touts your team's accomplishments, passions, tastes and whatever else you like.

Chapter 8:

Pinterest Contests Made Supremely Easy

"A business absolutely devoted to service will have only one worry about profits. They will be embarrassingly large."

-Henry Ford

Everyone loves to win FREE stuff. Everybody.

And throw in the rather low barrier-to-entry of a Pinterest contest — you ain't asking people to write an essay, all they gotta do is upload a picture or create a board — and you've got the perfect marketing engine to attract tons of followers, boost your brand awareness and turn those freebie-seekers into paying customers who buy your wares.

But there's a new Pinterest sheriff in town.

And the old "Pin It to Win It" model of Pinterest contests is being phased out. Because Pinterest thinks these type of contests are spammy. (They're right.)

So, before we dig into the nuts-and-bolts of your Pinterest contest campaign let's go over what you CAN'T do:

☑ Require people to "pin" your contest guidelines. (Big no-no)

☑ Run a contest where pinners vote with likes, pins or repins.

☑ Require people pin a single image, or a selection of images, to enter the contest.

☑ Set up a contest where each follow, pin, or repin represents a single entry.

☑ Suggest, in any way, that Pinterest endorses your contest.

Well, that kinda puts a crimp in things, don't it?

Don't worry.

All it did was kick the Internet hucksters out. (And leave room for us ethical marketers.)

So, here are my SIX Tips for Running a Super-Effective Pinterest Contest:

Pinterest Contest Tip No.1: Set Your Goals

I know. Setting social media goals is about as much fun as filing a tax return.

But without a clear set of goals for your Pinterest contest — that you and your team understand beforehand — you'll be unsure of:

a. How long to run the contest

b. What kind of prize to offer

c. How much money in advertising to put behind it… (Yes, it's possible you may have to spend a bit of money to spread the word about your Pinterest contest. But it'll be worth it.)

Here are some of the more common Pinterest contest goals that marketers have used successfully:

☑ Increasing your number of Pinterest followers

☑ Finding more subscribers for your email list

☑ Promoting an upcoming product launch

☑ Getting some publicity for your brand, product, service or cause

☑ Procuring some feedback for…well…almost anything

☑ Simply boosting the amount of traffic to your website

☑ And…of course…selling more stuff!

In my (not-so-humble) experience, the goals that I've had the most success with are getting more Pinterest followers, building up my email subscriber base and promoting a product launch.

I've had less success with getting "publicity" — whatever that means — and I find trying to simply sell more stuff hasn't worked out super well for me. (But I don't move in the e-commerce space. If you sell physical products, you shouldn't have any problem.)

And it's okay to have more than one goal with your Pinterest contest. But tread lightly…

Having more than two, maybe three, contest goals can water down your marketing efforts significantly. Don't worry, you can always run another contest next month to achieve different goals.

PINTEREST CONTEST TIP NO.2: GET CREATIVE WITH YOUR CONCEPT

This is where you get to flex your real marketing muscle. You just can't roll out the good-old "Pin It to Win It" contest model. It just means we need to be a little more creative, is all.

Here are a couple of contest concepts I've had REAL gains with:

☑ **Have users upload a photo or video of themselves** using your product, or doing something related to your business.

☑ Create a board where users can come up with the most creative/interesting/funny/heartfelt idea for a specific project or topic. (People love to feel like they're part of your behind-the-scenes brainstorming.)

☑ **Have users "vote" on two prospective products or projects**. Make sure the winning product or project is offered on discount. (And a couple of lucky winners get the item for free.)

☑ **Have users create their OWN board around a theme of your choosing**. Carnival Cruise Lines had great success with this when they asked users to create four boards related to four different dream destinations. (If only their maintenance crew was as innovative.)

☑ **Have users FIND missing pieces of a pinboard puzzle**, somewhere on your website. Audi crushed this when they showed close-up images of a car, and had people search their website for pictures that would fill in the rest of the automobile.

PINTEREST CONTEST TIP No.3: DECIDE ON THE RULES

This is really just a matter of working out how long the contest is going to be (I recommend a week, no longer), what people need to do to win the contest and whether you are running a "sweepstakes" or a "merit-based contest."

In case you're a little rusty on your contest terminology, a **sweepstakes** is where somebody enters a contest and a winner is chosen at random.

A **merit-based contest** is where somebody performs an action, such as uploading a video or creating a board, and then the contest organizer picks the winner.

Both are great. Both work really well.

If you're running a sweepstakes, you just want to be careful you don't run afoul of Pinterest terms of service. (You can get all their info at: http://business.pinterest.com/brand-guide-lines/)

As for what you should have entrants do, you could have them:

☑ Create boards

☑ Opt-in to your email list

☑ Follow your account

☑ Follow a specific board

☑ Upload a photo or video

I usually do a combination of things. Have them FOLLOW me and enter their email address. (Or have them upload a photo or video.)

Just make sure you get some way to market to the entrants in the future. (Email is STILL my favorite way to go here.)

PINTEREST CONTEST TIP NO.4: COME UP WITH A PRIZE THAT DOESN'T SUCK

This will depend heavily on what type of business you have, and what kind of targeted lead you are trying to acquire.

Obviously if you're marketing to PR professionals than a one-hour coaching call might be something those folks would be into.

But if you're trying to reach a "non-marketing" population, then the idea of talking "marketing" for an hour may sound like CIA interrogation.

Just put yourself in your user's point of view. What would be cool to them?

☑ A one-year supply of Greek yogurt?

☑ A master bedroom set?

☑ A big-screen TV?

☑ A subscription to the Smithsonian Magazine?

☑ A candlelight dinner with Justin Bieber?

Whatever you do, keep the prize simple enough to understand that it can be explained in a single image.

A Victoria's Secret gift card is pretty self-explanatory. (And in my wife's case…pretty awesome.) A TCP/IP corporate network security firewall is not.

PINTEREST CONTEST TIP No.5: OUTSOURCE THE ANXIETY

Right now, I'm going to share with you my secret weapon when it comes to Pinterest contests.

I don't handle any of it.

Really, most of the heavy lifting is done by an awesome, innovative company called Wishpond.

They are basically the go-to company when it comes to social media contests and sweepstakes. Note: It's not a free tool, but I'm a frequent customer, so they've set me up a link where you cool folks can get a FREE two-week trial over at http://punkrockmarketing.com/wishpond.

I love Wishpond because their tools offer:

☑ **Eye-catching imagery** you can use to promote your contest.

☑ **Custom entry forms**. (Works great for email opt-in forms.)

☑ **Sweepstakes compliance**. (So you don't have to deal with any of the boring legal stuff.)

☑ **Templates that make you look like an awesome web designer.** (Even if you aren't.)

☑ **The ability to "schedule" your contests** in advance. (I've run contests while sitting on a beach in Oahu.)

☑ **Landing-page templates that are mobile-friendly.** (This is huge!)

☑ **The ability to set up follow-up emails** and customize entrant's messages to their friends.

☑ **Killer analytics** to let you know what's working. (And what's not!)

☑ **The ability to promote your contest** on Twitter and Facebook easily.

And if you're extremely cheap, like I am, you can always run a 7-day contest within your two-week FREE trial and get all the benefit, without any of the cost.

PINTEREST CONTEST TIP No.6: PROMOTE THE CONTEST EVERYWHERE

Bit of a no-brainer, this one. But still true. Promote your contest on:

☑ Twitter

☑ Facebook

☑ Instagram

☑ Your Blog

☑ YouTube

☑ Press Release

☑ Email Newsletter

…anywhere you can think of! (Again, if the prize is good, and the contest is creative, you WILL get a great response.)

And you may suddenly have thousands of new leads, for the price of a Victoria's Secret gift card.

CHAPTER 8 KEY TAKEAWAYS:

☑ Come up with contest goals first. Are you going after new followers, new email subscribers…or simply trying to get press attention? Decide on goals, then come up with a strategy.

☑ Go beyond the usual. Come up with a creative concept that asks people to do MORE than just create a board or pin an item from your website.

☑ Lay down the law. Come up with the rules of the contest. (And make sure, if it's a sweepstakes, you follow Pinterest terms of service.)

☑ Find a quality prize. Bonus points if it fits in with the area of your company's expertise.

☑ Let somebody else handle the contest. Choose a tool like Wish-Pond to handle all the tech-y stuff associated with your contest.

☑ Promote! Spread the word about your contest on your blog, Twitter feed, YouTube Channel, Facebook page…anywhere that you can think of.

Chapter 9:

Standing on the Shoulders of Giants

"The mind is not a vessel to be filled, but a fire to be kindled."

-Plutarch

WORDS can only do so much.

I've tried to share some of the tips and tricks I've learned (the hard way) about how to turn all those pins and repins and boards of the Pinterest universe into actual money.

But sometimes, you just gotta SEE it.

So, in this final chapter, I'm going to share with you some companies I think are doing a GREAT job on Pinterest, and in particular, what area of Pinterest I think they are really killing it in.

Don't be intimidated if some of them are big brands and huge companies. There are plenty of big companies who suck at Pinterest, if they have any Pinterest presence at all.

Just start collecting ideas that you can use for your own Pinterest marketing efforts, and before you know it, you might be one of the big guys yourself.

Pinterst All-Star No.1: Chobani Greek Yogurt

The company that made Greek yogurt a national phenomenon knows what it's doing with Pinterest.

Not only do they have boards that extoll the many benefits of Greek yogurt — it's healthy for you ("Fit With It" board), it's great baked ("Baked With Chobani"), it's awesome frozen ("Chilly Chobani") — but they also do a fantastic job of recognizing their fans ("Chobani Champions") and creating nuggets of inspiration that have nothing to do with yogurt ("Nothing But Good" and "Go Real").

All-Star Resource: http://pinterest.com/chobani

Pinterest All-Star No.2: Etsy

Etsy, the handcraft marketplace that revived more craft rooms in America than the glue gun, was made for Pinterest and its visual revolution.

Of course, Etsy has plenty of themed boards that show off their awesome wares — ("Etsy Jewelry," "Cool Spaces", "DIY Projects") — but they also utilize the guest contributor feature quite well, with their series of "Guest Pinner" boards.

Also, the "Etsy Kids" and "Etsy Weddings" boards show this company ain't just about buying cool, handmade stuff made in a rural Pennsylvania farmhouse.

It's about being creative, and teaching the next generation that not everything should be made in a factory overseas.

All-Star Resource: http://pinterest.com/etsy

Pinterest All-Star No.3: Gap

The company who can't seem to decide on a logo, actually has a pretty good Pinterest strategy in place.

They don't have a ton of boards, but the ones they do have do a lot more than just show off the latest back-to-school styles.

Gap does a great job of getting their followers to post pictures of themselves wearing Gap clothing ("Styld.by You") and they've also created a clever board, called "GAPgrams," where users put their Gap outfits together in anthropomorphic poses…and then share them on Instagram. (Sounds weird, but it totally works.)

All-Star Resource: http://pinterest.com/gap

Pinterest All-Star No.4: Whole Foods Market

They call it food porn for a reason. But the Whole Foods Pinterest page offers a lot more than pretty pictures of soy burgers and seaweed grass smoothies.

It also offers fitness and nutrition tips for kids ("Kids: MOVE That Body," "A LunchBox That's Tops"), creative holiday boards ("Creative Christmas Projects"; "Spring Gatherings"), information on the company itself ("#WhyAustin") and the most popular of all, a board that allows followers to express their thanks for the role food plays in their life ("#foodthanks").

All-Star Resource: http://www.pinterest.com/wholefoods/

Epilogue:
A Final Note...

If the Internet is still in its infancy. Then Pinterest is in its first trimester.

It's still not clear how things will shake out for Pinterest.

- ☑ Will external websites get pissed off Pinterest is monopolizing their traffic? (Flickr sure is mad. Wonder who's next?)
- ☑ Will Pinterest start to charge users to use their service?
- ☑ Will they push paid placement like Facebook, Twitter and Instagram have?

What we do know, due to its overwhelmingly quick rise up the social media charts, is that Pinterest has hit a NERVE.

And that **nerve** is all about photos and videos that inspire people.

So, as you dip your toe into the Pinterest marketing waters, remember though the tactics of this super-trendy social network may change...

The strategy is here to stay.

- ☑ Keep it visual.
- ☑ Keep it simple.
- ☑ Keep it positive.

I have real doubts that people will read longform text on a screen in the future. (And as an English major, that mortally offends me.)

But the more you can present the story of your company in a simple, compelling image…

…the more your business will be poised to not just **survive** these crazy, chaotic economic times.

But actually thrive. (And what could be more inspiring and motivating than that.)

Here's hoping YOU thrive and kick some serious ass in your Pinterest efforts.

*   *   *

Paranoid over Pinterest? Puh-lease!

To grab your very own FREE Pinterest Marketing Cheat Sheet, head over to **PunkRockMarketing.com** TODAY and get instant access to your very own Pinterest marketing checklist.

It's so easy, Martha Stewart can do it without violating parole.

Again, head over to PunkRockMarketing.com TODAY and get your FREE Pinterest Marketing Cheat Sheet.

And if you have any questions, just drop me a line at Michael@punkrockmarketing.com.

Okay...this is where we put it all together, young Jedi. Because now you're prepared for...

Michael Clarke

EMAIL
MARKETING
THAT
DOESN'T SUCK

Vol.5
of the Punk Rock
Marketing
COLLECTION

Prologue:
Email Marketing is Dead, Long Live Email Marketing

Got a question for ya…

Why the hell are you reading this section of the book?

I mean it.

Didn't you get the memo?

…that email is old-fashioned?

Behind the times.

Something your grandmother uses to send you the latest chain-letter message she came across. ("Look out, dear. The government is keeping your emails in a vault in Cleveland.")

That it's impossible to make money with email marketing when:

- ☑ Email open rates are down.
- ☑ Email click-through-rates are WAY down.
- ☑ Email conversions are abysmal.
- ☑ Email providers, like Gmail, keep changing the rules and making things terminally impossible for us hustlers trying to make a buc.

And that in a world of tweets and likes and pins and status updates, that email is the 21st-century version of the rotary phone. (Quaint, but obsolete.)

'Cept…

Have you noticed when those nifty social-networking tools want to let you know about those tweets and likes and pins and status updates they're dying to share with you...

...they send you EMAILS.

Still.

So, while it's true email marketing doesn't work quite as well for most marketeres.

It isn't because the medium is dead. (It's that most marketers don't have any idea what the hell they're doing.)

And if you KNOW what you're doing, if you tell stories and talk to people like humans...

...instead of chirping on and on like some drone in a robot-marketing army...

Then not only can you make email marketing a cheap, cost-effective part of your marketing arsenal, but you will dramatically stand out from the rest of the morons in your business niche.

And by following the tips in this book, your customers will actually look forward to your emails. (I know! Crazy, right?)

When that happens, you'll be scooping in so much new business and raking in so much extra moolah...

...that you might even have the funds to make that investment the Finance Minister of Nigeria emailed you about.

Alright...let's get this (email) party started!

Chapter 1:

3 Things You Absolutely, Positively Gotta Have

"Give me six hours to chop down a tree and I will spend the first four sharpening the axe."

-Abraham Lincoln

We're going to get to the nuts-and-bolts of email marketing: "What do I write, when do I send it, and how do I get people to buy my crap?"

Promise.

But before we do that, we need to make sure you are armed and ready to do serious email marketing battle. (And not, to quote one of my favorites movies of all times, bringing a "knife to a gunfight.")

So, here are my Top THREE Email Marketing Tools you gotta, gotta, gotta have before you can crush the competition with your email marketing awesomeness:

MUST-HAVE TOOL NO.1: AUTORESPONDER SERVICE (PAID)

An autoresponder service, such as AWeber (http://punkrockmarketing.com/aweber) or iContact (http://punkrockmarketing.com/icontact) or InfusionSoft (http://punkrockmarketing.com/infusionsoft) — there are many — does a ton of cool things you absolutely NEED to kill it with email marketing:

a. **Handles ALL your mass email sends** (so your regular email account doesn't get banned by sending out hundreds of emails at the same time.)

b. **Drastically IMPROVES your open rates and delivery rates**. (They work hard to remove blacklists that anal email service providers just love to use.)

c. **Lets you write your welcome emails** and follow-up emails months, if not years, in advance. (THIS. IS. HUGE.)

d. **Lets you AUTOMATICALLY add people** to your email list if they buy something from you.

e. **Provides a ton of email templates** that let you send out CUSTOMIZED and super-visually interesting newsletters and emails.

f. **Provides you some nifty little CODE** you can put on your website or blog, so you don't have to handle any of the email addresses yourself.

Some autoresponder services, such as 1 Shopping Cart, even let you have e-commerce checkout system baked into your account.

My personal weapon of choice is AWeber. (The cost is $20 a month for up to 10K subscribers, and then it goes from up there. But they offer a 30-day trial to let you give it a test-drive for only a buck.)

Just make sure you STICK with whatever service you choose to go with. Switching over to another service can be a real pain in the email ass.

Must-Have Tool No.2: A Landing Page That Doesn't Suck (Free or Paid)

And by doesn't suck, I mean a landing page, with an email opt-in form that converts pretty well. (And by pretty well, I mean somewhere in the 20-35% range.)

Most marketers have landing pages that suck because they:

- ☑ **Put too much CRAP on their page**. The Landing Page should do one thing. Ask for an email address. (Not SELL your entire line of KISS memorabilia.)
- ☑ **Their landing page is UG-LY**. Looks like it came out of an AOL members' page in the mid-90s.
- ☑ **They have their email opt-in BELOW the fold**. People gotta scroll down to see it, and getting people to "scroll down" for a FREE iPad is a chore.
- ☑ **They DON'T tell people what they'll get by opting-in.**
- ☑ **They focus on features, NOT benefits**. People don't buy the All-Wheel Steering. They buy the FEELING of driving like James Bond.
- ☑ **Their headline is BORING** and sucky.

Now, the last three points touch on the rather involved craft of copywriting. (I don't have room to go into the complete ins and outs of copywriting here, but there are a ton of good books on the subject. My favorite is "The Copywriter's Handbook," by Robert Bly - http://punkrockmarketing.com/copywriter.)

As for how your landing page LOOKS, my favorite weapon — no matter whether your site is on WordPress or not — is a tool called Lead Pages (http://punkrockmarketing.com/lead).

This thing comes LOADED with a bunch of templates to outfit your squeeze pages, sales pages and membership pages.

In addition, it's dead easy to use. (And they handle all the split testing for you. No need to fuss with code.)

Trust me, this tool'll make you look more talented and smarter than you actually are.

If you're on a serious budget then try having a designer code something up for you at oDesk (http://punkrock-marketing.com/odesk) or Elance (http://punkrockmar-keting.com/elance), both of these sites have plenty of talented, but underworked, web professionals who can hook you up.

Just make sure:

☑ **The page is responsive.** (Meaning it works on a mobile device.)

☑ **The page has one simple Call-to-Action**, not 25 things the user can do.

☑ **The page has an image (or video) and an opt-in box**. (And not much else.)

MUST-HAVE TOOL NO.3: A COOL, FREE THING YOU'RE GIVING AWAY

As marketers, we may believe that asking folks to hand over their email address is NO BIG DEAL.

But our (future) customers don't see it that way.

Most people KNOW that giving their email address to somebody may lead to:

☑ A clogged email inbox

☑ Annoying, spammy emails they don't want in the first place

☑ Tough decisions (Such as: "Do I buy this thing from this person I've never heard of?")

So, if you're going to ask people for an email address, make sure you give them something COOL in return.

Like a FREE eBook, video, report, CD, Cheat Sheet, Insider's Guide or a NEW CAR! Something!

Not only does it act as a flavorful carrot to entice people to give you their email digits…

…but, let's say, you actually do a halfway-decent job of delivering quality content in your FREE THING…

…they'll be BLOWN AWAY. They'll:

- ☑ Think you're an awesome trustworthy human person. (Instead of a shady marketer.)

- ☑ Want to read your emails. (Which makes marketing your emails that much easier.)

- ☑ Be way more likely to BUY something from you.

So, what kind of freebie (or "lead magnet" as the hipsters call it) should you give away?

I think that entirely depends on what your strengths are.

If you like writing, then I'd do an eBook or report.

If you like video, then a screen-capture vid or talking-head video would be good.

If you're more graphical, then maybe an infographic or PowerPoint presentation would be right up your alley. Infogram (http://infogr.am) is my favorite place to create infographics for FREE.

The HOW is not as important as the WHAT, which should be some form of:

- ☑ Cheat sheet

- ☑ Insider guide

- ☑ Mini-Course

☑ Tip, or series of tips

☑ A solution to a problem

People are lazy. And the more you provide easy solutions to hard things, the more you'll be able to convince total strangers to give you their email address. (And their money.)

CHAPTER 1 KEY TAKEAWAYS:

☑ Sign up for an autoresponder service such as AWeber to handle all your email deliver-ability needs.

☑ Make sure your landing page does one thing: collects email addresses. (Use a tool like Lead Pages to make it look super pretty, and mobile-friendly.)

☑ Give something FREE away, so people will opt-in to your email list, instead of just offering a crappy newsletter that nobody wants.

☑ Boost your headline and copywriting game by picking up a book such as "The Copywriter's Handbook."

☑ Create a nifty, cool FREE thing to give away to your email subscribers, such as a cheat sheet, insider's guide, training video, or mini-course.

Chapter 2:

How to Get Tons of Subscribers...FAST!

"Only those who risk going too far can possibly find out how far one can go."

-T.S. Eliot

Okay, so ya got your email-marketing tools set up!

Hopefully by this point you've:

- ☑ Signed up for an autoresponder service.
- ☑ Placed some code (courtesy of your autoresponder company) on your website that will let people "opt-in" to your email list.
- ☑ Created some enticing FREEBIE that people actually want...and will happily give over their email address to get access to.

So, once you've got those things crossed off your list, it's now time to go out there and get some good old subscribers to your email list.

So, here are my FIVE Super-Ninja Email Subscriber Methods:

Email Subscriber Method No.1: Video (and Lots of It)

Not only is video cool, and makes you look like a total expert, even if you aren't, but it also converts really well (In some of my markets, my YouTube videos convert at nearly a 60% rate. That's huge!)

The keys are:

1. **Make sure your videos solve people's problems, and don't overtly sell.** People don't like straight-up marketing messages and YouTube will probably crack down on overly promo videos at some point.

2. **Choose video titles that incorporate SEO-friendly keywords.** Opt for "How to Clean a Jacuzzi," NOT "Joe's Pool Supply Tips".

3. **Have a clear Call-to-Action that mentions your FREEBIE in the Video.** This means you need to tell people what to do when the video ends. Like, "Head over to my website NOW and get this free thing!"

4. **Promote first!** Have the first thing in your video description be a LINK to your FREEBIE. Most people won't hit the "more" button and see the rest of your description. (And you'll miss out on a possible chance to create a new lead.)

5. **Ask viewers to do things.** Such as: Facebook Like, Retweet and give a Thumbs Up to your videos. (Having all this social activity swirling around your videos make them much more visible.)

Email Subscriber Method No.2: Tweet a Link to Your FREEBIE

This one's a no-brainer. And yet, so many marketers neglect it. (I guess they've got more important stuff to do on Twitter. Like, find out what Kim Kardashian is wearing.)

At least once a week tweet out a link to your FREE lead magnet. Just be sure to tweet out other non-promotional stuff the rest of the week, so you don't come off like some kind of Twitter spammer.

Here are a couple ways to get the most out of these freebie tweets:

☑ **Mention the word FREE…in all CAPS.** There's a reason it's the most powerful word in the English language.

☑ **Mention a specific benefit of your FREEBIE,** not just the FREEBIE itself. Go with — "FREE guide shows how not to get ripped off when you buy a new car" instead of "Download this 67-page guide today."

☑ **Ask people to RT (Retweet).** People on social media are lemmings and will do what you tell them to do. So tell'em to share your tweet.

EMAIL SUBSCRIBER METHOD NO.3: FACEBOOK ADS

I have had huge success using Facebook ads in building up my email list.

Facebook page status updates…eh…not so much!

I find Facebook Page status updates are great conversation starters, good for getting people to talk about something. (Usually themselves.) Not so awesome for getting people to plunk over their email info.

But creating a little custom tab on your Facebook Page that gives people the chance to sign up for your email list is a super effective, and way cheaper, method for building up your email list.

Couple things to keep in mind:

☑ **Send Facebook ad traffic back to a tab** on your Facebook page. NOT to your website. Conversion rates royally suck when you send people out of the Facebook universe.

- ☑ **Target fans of your competitors**. Super sneaky way to get to their customer base. (And they are probably doing the same to you, anyway.)

- ☑ **The more "activity" your Facebook page has, the cheaper your ad costs will be**. So keep doing all that crazy social media stuff while you run your ads. (It will help keep your cost-per-lead down.)

EMAIL SUBSCRIBER METHOD NO.4: PPC TRAFFIC

In case you aren't familiar with the term, PPC stands for Pay-Per-Click marketing. And it refers to those ANNOY-ING ads you see on search engines, like Google or Bing, that are positioned right above the results you ACTUALLY care about.

And, yes, it's true. People do click on these.

The way you buy that ad inventory is by bidding on certain *keywords* such as "quit smoking" or "used baseball mitt" through ad platorms such as Google AdWords or the Yahoo/Bing Ad Network.

PPC traffic can be good. And very profitable. (These are people looking to solve problems.)

It can also make you broke, fast, if you're not careful.

I am by no means a PPC expert; there are way more quali-fied left-brained folks out there. But here's what I've learned, the hard way, with running PPC campaigns:

- ☑ **Stick with "long" (3-5 word) -phrases**. Skip "weight loss" and go for "how to fit in a prom dress." Cheaper and more profitable.

☑ **Go with phrases that seem to have a commercial intent.** (Meaning people will spend money on it.) "Free ringtones" ain't a winner. But "Lady Gaga ringtones" might be more up your alley.

☑ **Make sure your website landing page has a good amount of content on there.** This'll keep your PPC costs low. Now, you don't have to write a book, but maybe throw in 200 or so informative words about that specific keyword, to keep the Google police off your back.

EMAIL SUBSCRIBER METHOD NO.5: FINDING LEADS ANYWHERE YOU CAN

Whenever I'm building a new email list, I generally like to create opt-in opportunities anywhere I can.

So here are a couple of my favorite — both online and offline — ways to find new email subscribers:

☑ **Put a notice on the store counter.** If ya got a brick-and-mortar business, this is a must.

☑ **Every single "About Me" field in every social media profile I can think of.** This includes my YouTube channel, my Pinterest pin board, my Facebook profile, and my Twitter bio. Wherever you can, throw in a link to a website landing page.

☑ **Message board and forum signatures.** You don't want to spam folks, but if you answer questions in a relevant online forum, and then have a link in your forum signature to your FREEBIE, people will check it out.

☑ **Press releases.** This one can be a surprisingly consistent form of steady traffic.

☑ **An opt-in box on your "checkout page."** This can actually help convert visitors into buyers. (Weird, I know. But it totally works.) And things that work, give me more time to do things I love.

Like buy more Lady Gaga ringtones.

CHAPTER 2 KEY TAKEAWAYS:

☑ Create YouTube videos, with keyword-friendly titles, to send traffic back to your landing page.

☑ Tweet out a link to your FREE THING a couple times a week on Twitter.

☑ Use Facebook ads to drive traffic to a custom tab on your fan page that lets people opt-in to your list.

☑ Dip your toe into the PPC world. But be sure to stick to long-tail keywords that keep out the freebie seekers.

☑ Put a link to your landing page everywhere — both online and offline — that you can think of.

Chapter 3:

My Ultimate Email Marketing Formula

"Make a customer, not a sale."

Katherine Barchetti

Most business folks — even those with high-priced degrees from impressive academic institutions — usually drop the ball when it comes to email marketing.

And that's because they do one of THREE things:

1. **They sell way too early** (and sell too much) in the email marketing process.

2. **They send out episodic emails** that have no connection to each other.

3. **They email their subscribers WAY TOO MUCH**. (Or not NEARLY ENOUGH.)

This is known as the *"Till They Buy or Die"* philosophy.

The system goes something like this:

1. Add tons of people to your email list.

2. Send them an email every couple days selling your latest "thing."

3. Keep sending them emails until they unsubscribe or buy something.

And, sure, if you've got a big enough email list, and an un-limited budget, this can totally work.

But it can be REALLY EXPENSIVE.

And if you constantly harass your readers with emails pitching crap they don't want, then you'll have an extremely high rate of churn.

And you won't be able to take advantage of long-term (1 year+) email relationships with your customers. Any successful marketer will tell you, long-term customers are where the REAL MONEY is.

So, how do we avoid those mistakes?

How do we make the most of your lead-acquisition budget and build dedicated, consistent customers who give us money over and over again?

How do we develop long-term customers who feel connected to us and respond consistently to our email marketing?

We stop marketing so damn much, of course.

THE PUNK ROCK EMAIL MARKETING FORMULA

I can't take all the credit for this approach. (Even though I really want to.)

One of the absolute masters of email marketing is Andre Chaperon. (If ya want an absolute Ph.D. in email marketing that absolutely crushes, check out his Autoresponder Madness course - http://punkrockmarketing.com/auto. It's worth every penny.)

But here's the bare-bones formula in a nutshell.

We start off by giving each new email subscriber an initial sequence of emails that slowly tell a story and build our credibility by positioning ourselves as somebody who doesn't just want to sell crap, but actually cares whether they succeed or fail.

And then we transition them slowly into a more spaced-out, weekly email schedule.

A good calendar would look something like below. I'll share my formula with more detail in the following chapter (it looks a little different, but the same principle…you gotta find what works for you!)

Phase 1: The Initial "Get to Know Ya" Sequence

Day 1- Day 5: An email every day that gives your subscribers a tip, solution, or story that relates to their problem/need. (We don't SELL ANYTHING directly during this time. But we do provide Resource Links at the bottom of our emails where people can always buy stuff if they want.)

Day 6: We offer them something to buy. (But in a cool, not super obvious way.)

Day 7- Day 21: An email EVERY THREE DAYS that gives people more tips, more solutions, more stories.

Day 22: We offer them another something to buy. (Could be our product, or somebody else's.)

Phase 2: Infinity and Beyond

Day 23-End of Time: We send them a weekly email, which goes out to our entire list, talking about some recent tip or story that can help them with their lives.

Phase 3: The Sales Sequence

Occasionally, no more than once a month, we will have something to sell. (Something different than what we've already offered them.)

To do this we will send them THREE EMAILS over the course of THREE DAYS. The first TWO emails setting the stage for the THIRD email where we actually offer them something to buy.

WHY THIS SYSTEM WORKS

Okay, so before you freak out and say: "I can't do this! That's way too much work. I'll never be able to pull this off."

A few things:

1. **Yeah, it's work.** That's why nobody else does it.

2. **The initial sequence gets rid of freebie seekers by the sheer volume of email.** And if that's what they are, you don't want them on your list anyway.

3. **Don't think of it as TEN TIPS or TEN STORIES.** Instead, think of it as one extended story with ten episodes. (In the next chapter, I'll talk more about how to pull this off.)

4. **You don't have to do it ALL at once.** You can write, and rewrite, and tweak as you go. (Slowly building up your catalog of emails.)

5. **The emails don't have to be long.** Maybe 200-500 words apiece.

6. **The 21 days is deliberate.** It takes 21 days for somebody to develop a habit. In this case, YOU are the new habit.)

7. **You will give your readers tons of opportunities to BUY STUFF.** It just won't feel like you're hounding them 24-7.

8. **I repeat...nobody does this.** To your new leads they will be astounded that somebody took the time and care to help them out this much, without "selling" so much. (And the concept of "obligation" is hard-wired

in the human brain. At some point, a very large amount of people will BUY something.)

And that "something" might as well be your product or service.

CHAPTER 3 KEY TAKEAWAYS:

- ☑ Don't sell, tell stories. Most email marketers make the huge mistake of SELLING from the get-go, and by sending out emails that have no context or logical sequence.

- ☑ Start off with an initial sequence for the first 21 days that emphasizes content-only emails and infrequent sales offers.

- ☑ After 21 days, we recommend shifting to a weekly-email format.

- ☑ This works because: nobody else does it and it conditions your subscribers to look forward to your emails while building up the feeling of obligation in your subscribers.

Chapter 4:

Initial Sequence or How Not to Be a Stalker

"The beautiful part of writing is that you don't have to get it right the first time, unlike, say, brain surgery."

-Robert Cormier

There's nothing quite like the first week of a romance.

The sun shines a little brighter. The birds sing a little louder. And the world feels like it's all unicorns and rainbows…

I remember once meeting this beautiful, slightly crazy, punk-rock girl who worked at my local neighborhood used-record store.

After chatting for awhile, I realized we had SO MUCH in common. ("Wait, you mean you love late 70's British punk and have a slightly irrational fear of clowns? Me too!")

Things were going great, until halfway through our SEC-OND DATE, when she asked if I could chip in for the security deposit on a new apartment, as it was pretty likely I'd be moving in soon.

We didn't have a third date.

"You Had Me at Hello"

And that's just what happens when you ask somebody to give you money the first or second or third time they get an email from you.

That FIRST WEEK of your email "relationship" with your subscribers is CRUCIAL. It sets the tone for the entire life of your (email) conversation.

It cements in their mind whether you're in their corner, and truly want them to succeed, or you're just like every other huckster out there.

Because to most of your subscribers, they have NO IDEA who the hell you are.

It's one thing for Amazon, WalMart, Tony Robbins or Oprah Winfrey to pitch something in the first week of "gettin' to know ya" emails.

But last time I checked, you and I don't walk on fire or give away cars to a studio audience.

We're marketers, and we've got to do WAY more romancing and courting than Overstock.com.

And that involves selling less of our crap and telling more really cool stories. (Ironically, if you tell good stories, you end up selling way more stuff.)

So, here is a closer look at how I approach each of my email marketing campaigns…

…and how I've used this very same system to sell products and services in markets as diverse as self-publishing, golf and even the restaurant business.

Day 1- Day 6: The First Story (One Email Every Day for Six Days)

This is where you explore the PAIN your subscribers have, and how it relates to the FREE LEAD MAGNET you created.

Then, at the end of the story, you give them a chance to buy something really cool from you.

I would structure things like this:

Email 1:

☑ Welcome them to your universe

☑ Give them a bit of background on YOU

☑ Give them reasons as to why they should listen to you

☑ Tell them what they can expect from you over the course of the next couple of emails

Email 2:

☑ Acknowledge their pain

☑ Give them a Quick Tip (and I mean QUICK) to help them solve their most immediate, pressing problem

Email 3:

☑ Talk about common obstacles/objections your ideal customer might have taking the next step. (Hearing these articulated will be huge for your subscribers.)

☑ Bonus: Throw in mistakes you've made, things you've learned, ways your new subscriber can take shortcuts and save time. (This is like crack to your subscribers.)

Email 4:

☑ Give them a concrete example of somebody who has used your WIDGET or SERVICE or COMPANY and been really happy with it.

☑ Don't sell, just tell the story! You don't even have to mention the WIDGET or SERVICE yet, but hint that there IS a solution.

Email 5:

☑ List a couple of benefits/features your product has — this is the first time you've mentioned it — and why it might be a good fit for them. (Don't overtly sell.)

Email 6:

☑ Tell them the product/service is now available. And give them reasons why it's urgent they get it now. (Limited supply, limited-time offer, their life will be shallow and empty if they don't get it right NOW.)

Now, before you run off and write your SIX EMAILS about how wonderful your WIDGET IS:

☑ **Keep these emails short, but not too short.** (More on this later.) A good page to a page and a half (double spaced) in MS Word is a good barometer.

☑ **Write them from the point of view of a PERSON.** I had success writing a campaign from the POV of my mom. (Boy, was that strange.) Emotions sell way more than logical, boring arguments.

☑ **Put links at the bottom of your emails to your PRODUCT SALES PAGE.** (Some people will click, trust me.) But DON'T overtly sell until Email #6.

☑ **Again, don't forget to put in mistakes you've made**, or other people have made, and how your readers can avoid them. People just LOVE reading about these.

☑ **And the MOST IMPORTANT RULE OF ALL**: Be sure to tease the end of each email, talking about the next one. (More on this in Chapter 6.)

☑ **Don't worry about what days of the week to send these emails**. Just send them in sequence and trust people will be interested in your stuff. But I recommend scheduling them in the morning, about 3:00 a.m.-6:00 a.m. local time for the subscriber. (All the major autoresponder services let you do this.)

DAY 9- DAY 22: STORY CYCLE #2

So, at this point, people have gone through your first story.

Just because they didn't buy doesn't mean they don't want to hear from you. (Don't worry, they'll unsubscribe or make a spam complaint if they don't want to hear from you.)

Perhaps the thing you were offering just didn't appeal to them. Now, it's time for story cycle two.

It's similar to cycle one, but with some slight tweaks. For one thing, you're going to email them every three days. (It's good to give them a break right after you hit them with that first week.)

Again, this will lead to another product or service pitch at the end…

But here's what I like to do:

Email Day 9:

Write a quick email on the state of your industry. What you see as the future trends of your area of business. (This will brand you as the expert.)

Email Day 12:

This time write about what those future trends/changes in your industry mean for your reader. (We're going from the global to the more personal.)

Email Day 15:

Offer a Quick Tip addressing some of the challenges/obstacles your subscriber/customer faces going forward with these changes.

Email Day 18:

Give an example of how your product/service has helped SOMEBODY take on these challenges.

Email Day 21:

List the features/benefits of your PRODUCT.

Email Day 22:

Give them the sales pitch for your thing. Again, ramp up the urgency. (Limited supply, limited-time offer, or their life will be shallow and empty if they don't get it.)

Here are a couple of tips for **Story Cycle Two**:

☑ Make sure the product/service you are pitching in this story cycle is MORE EXPENSIVE than the first product/service. This is your marketing funnel and now you start ascending them up the chain.

☑ Put links at the bottom of each email to your product/service. Like before, just remember to hold off mentioning the product until email 21.

☑ Use the cliffhanger tease at the end of each email. Again.

☑ Don't worry about which days of the week to send these.

Though my conversion rates are generally lower for Story Cycle Two than they are for Story Cycle One, my profit margins are usually higher. (Because of the higher price point.)

But the cool thing is, once you write these 12 emails — I like to bust them out over a week or so — then they're done. You don't have to really touch them, unless you see that some of them aren't working. (More on that in Chapter 9.)

Then you can turn your attention to where the real big money is…that is the weekly emails. (Which we'll cover next.)

CHAPTER 4 KEY TAKEAWAYS:

- ☑ Email marketing is like a new relationship. So chill out, and don't be such a stalker at first.
- ☑ Write your emails from one person's point of view. Could be you, a former customer or Harry Potter.
- ☑ Focus on expressing pain and objections in Story Cycle One.
- ☑ Focus on setting yourself up as an expert, and voice in your industry, in Story Cycle Two.
- ☑ Offer a higher-priced item in Story Cycle Two.
- ☑ Don't forget to express urgency. They need your product or service NOW.

Chapter 5:

Zen and the Art of the Weekly Email

"We read to know we are not alone."

-William Nicholson

All right, we've come to the piece of email marketing that most people are familiar with.

And that's the weekly email blast which is sent to all, or a good portion, of your subscribers.

This can be in the form of a Newsletter, a Quick Tip, a Weekly Essay, an inbox magazine, or just your bitter, angry ramblings about a society gone awry. (I prefer the latter.)

The actual form of media isn't as important as the frequency. (Which is weekly.)

Does have it to be weekly? I mean, weekly is so much work and I've got things to do and there are all those episodes of "Rockford Files" on Netflix to catch up on…

'Fraid so.

I have found that anything less than weekly, actually hurts response rates and leads to a much higher rate of unsubscribes. People will literally forget they signed up for your newsletter minutes after opting-in to your list. Let alone THREE WEEKS later.

To get the consistent results you want, you'll need to keep putting yourself out there. And sending an email every month, or every couple of weeks, just won't help you reach your goals. (Trust me, people's inboxes are crowded and busy. It's much better to send TOO MUCH than not SEND ENOUGH.)

So, before you dig in your heels and start creating your weekly email editorial calendar, here are some guidelines to keep you on track when it comes to your weekly email marketing efforts:

What Should I Put in My Weekly Email?

Well, this will be entirely up to you and the business you're in. I like the newsletter/magazine format for many markets I'm in, which includes:

- ☑ A main message or quick tip.
- ☑ A spotlight on one of your email subscribers (people love these).
- ☑ A motivational quote (people love these even more).
- ☑ A link to recommended resources: Perhaps a weekly coupon or offer, or a link to your own products and services, or products you're an affiliate of.
- ☑ Social Media Icons at the bottom so people can stay "in touch" with you. Creepy, but effective.

Yeah, But Do I Have to Put All That Stuff in My Weekly Email?

No. You don't.

I have an email list which caters to CPAs. Motivational quotes don't really do much for them.

They just want the actionable tip and then want to get on

with their lives. (Which usually involves billing their clients hundreds of dollars an hour.)

But then I've also got an email list focusing on songwriters. That crowd loves quotes and anecdotes and recognition. Mostly because songwriters make slightly less than poets.

And if I were running a brick-and-mortar business, then I may want to just put in a weekly "Offer of the Week." (More on subject lines later.)

WHAT SHOULD MY WEEKLY EMAIL LOOK LIKE? (HOW PRETTY DOES IT NEED TO BE?)

I'm the world's worst graphic/web designer person. So I wouldn't want to give you stray advice on these matters.

But all of the autoresponder services I mentioned in Chapter 1 (AWeber, InfusionSoft, Mail Chimp) have a ton of easy-to-use templates to make your weekly email look as awesome or boring as you like.

Here are a few things I've learned, the hard way, about making your weekly emails all pretty:

- ☑ **Make your font big**. (At least 14-18px) Shows up better on mobile devices.
- ☑ **Don't go crazy with images**. Most will be blocked by email providers anyway.
- ☑ **If you do have an awesome HTML-designed newsletter**, be DAMN SURE you have a text-only version as well. (Most autoresponders will have this by default.)
- ☑ **Check your email on various devices and email clients**. The same email can look drastically different depending on which overpriced smartphone you're using.

WHEN DO I SEND IT?

Ah, yes. Send times.

There might be no bigger cause for debate in email marketing circles — yes, those circles do exist; and they are quite dorky — then when to send your weekly email blasts.

Some folks will tell you to avoid the weekends. (Because most people have their primary email tied to work.)

Other people will tell you Sunday mornings are great, because most people "catch up" on their emails then. (How sad is it we spend Sundays getting through our email backlog?)

I can only tell you what I've found in MY experience. (Feel free to test to figure out which send time is right for you.)

Here are my not-so-hard and fast rules about send times:

☑ **Avoid Mondays.** Most emails are sent this day. Engagement is high. But you're likely to get lost in the email shuffle.

☑ **Avoid Fridays.** People start to get email fatigue about Friday. (Which is not good for email marketers.)

☑ **Avoid Saturdays.** Too much going on.

☑ **Tuesdays-Thursdays are really good**. My personal favorite is Thursday, as people are generally "thinking" about the weekend already, which makes it easy to tap into their "escapist" mentality.

☑ **Sundays are good, but it depends on your market**. Open rates are generally down on Sundays. But CTR's (Click-Through-Rates are higher.) There's a lot less competition on Sundays, but you can sometimes get people skipping over your email, or reading it days later.

BUT I DON'T KNOW WHAT TO WRITE ABOUT!

A lot of email marketing gurus will tell you to come up with a list of the 20 most common questions/obstacles your customers have and just go down one-by-one and write an email about it.

And that works…okay. But I use something more nuanced.

Here's what I suggest:

☑ Come up with a list of problems/obstacles your email readers may be having/experiencing. Say your email list caters to contractors, it could be the rising cost of supplies, difficulty of finding good workers, truck maintenance issues, etc.

☑ Come up with a tip/solution/insight you have about that issue. Keep it focused and short.

☑ Tell a story about a person, either yourself, somebody on the team or one of your customers, who encountered that same problem.

☑ Give a happy ending/solution.

Notice the difference between these two:

VERSION 1:

"Finding reliable construction workers to add to your team can be a challenge.

"Despite a thorough screening process it can be difficult to find quality employees that match your company's needs.

"Here's a resource which may benefit your small business…"

VERSION 2:

"I got the call last Thursday at the job site.

"My tile guy wasn't gonna make it. He was sick. Or hungover. (Who knows?)

"Either way I was behind schedule, the client was mad and I was in danger of another horrible Angie's List review.

"But then I came across something that saved the day…"

See how different those read?

It's the same TIP, but a completely different emotional experience.)

And that's what you want with the weekly emails, emotional experiences.

I'm Confused. How Does the Weekly Email Work With the Initial Sequence?

Here's what happens, the moment somebody signs up for your list they get your initial sequence of emails. (We went over this in detail in Chapter 4.)

While that's playing out they will also get your weekly email blast.

Yes, there will be some overlap. Yes, some people will be knee-deep in your initial sequence, while they may get a few weekly emails.

That's okay. If it's too much for them, they'll un-subscribe. (Trust me.)

When the initial sequence plays out, then the weekly email blast will be the ongoing touch-point of our email marketing relationship.

Why Don't You Start With the Weekly Email Blast? Why Waste Time With the Initial Sequence?

Because the MOMENT somebody signs up for your email list they are at their most vulnerable.

They have a problem that needs solving. (Otherwise they wouldn't have found you.)

And while MOST of the world will be trying to sell them crap, you will — through the initial sequence — be taking them from confusion to solution.

Even if they don't buy from you in that sequence, they'll see you as somebody they can TRUST. Somebody who's in it for more than just the quick buck.

And when you do have something to sell, and the offer is something they are interested in, they will pounce on it. (Which is what we'll cover in the next chapter.)

CHAPTER 5 KEY TAKEAWAYS:

☑ You can put as little or as much in your weekly emails as you like.

☑ Common elements include:
  • a weekly tip
  • spotlight on a reader
  • recommended resources
  • social sharing icons
  • book reviews and recommended resources.

☑ Tuesdays-Thursdays are good days to send your weekly email, but Sundays can be good too, depending on the market.

☑ Write about solving people's problems, but from a personal POV. (Not dry, boring lectures.)

☑ It's okay if weekly emails and initial sequences overlap.

Chapter 6:

3 Steps to Huge Email Marketing Profits

"Your customer doesn't care how much you know until they know how much you care."

-Damon Richards

Finally, you're saying. We're gonna actually get to what I RE-ALLY care about.

Making some moolah!

Hold on there, Turbo.

At this point, you should already have made a ton of sales, through the links at the bottom of all your emails and from the direct pitches at the end of your initial sequence.

But, let's get one thing clear: The EMAIL, as a medium, is an exceptionally crappy way to make your sales pitch.

People SCAN emails. They don't really READ them with the attention and focus that's needed for a financial decision.

But…

…emails ARE really good for developing relationships. (Which is what we've done through the initial sequence and the weekly email.)

And, once you do have a product or service to sell folks, emails are a GREAT WAY to send people to a sales page on your website.

And before I show you an absolutely devastating way to make a ton of sales through emails, let's talk a bit about your sales page. (And make sure it's where it needs to be to set you up for success.)

A SUPER-QUICK GUERILLA GUIDE TO SALES PAGES

What should be on that sales page of yours?

Well, it's a bit beyond the scope of this book to cover every bit of sales-page techniques, but let me give you some quick down-and-dirty tips when using email to send your subscribers to a sales page.

☑ The headline is the most important part of the sales page. Keep it short.

☑ Make sure the headline is part of the conversation going on in your customer's head. Example: "Is your 401K in the crapper?" is better than "Training Course reveals things you should know about your 401K."

☑ Write 10 headlines. Then write 10 more. Pick the best one.

☑ If you can, do video. Converts much better than those super-long sales pages, and has a much better engagement rate.

☑ Follow the good-old formula of "Problem, Agitate, Solve." Example: **Problem:** *"As a business owner you know employee theft is an issue…"* **Agitate:** *"But you may not know that for every dollar you earn, 45 cents is walking out the door…"* **Solve:** *"Here's my patented system for catching employee thieves. It's called a pitbull."*

☑ Get as many testimonials as you can. Video testimonials work even better.

☑ As you write your copy, and/or record your video, think about the word: URGENCY. They need this NOW. Not later, NOW!

The Sales Trinity of Awesomeness

So, again, I didn't invent this here technique.

It's a bit of a hybrid between Internet marketer Frank Kern and the great work done by the aforementioned Andre Chaperon. (Again, if you want an Advanced Degree in Sales Emails check out his Autoresponder Madness - http://punkrockmarketing.com/auto.)

But the trinity goes something like this:

☑ Email 1: Feel Their Pain

☑ Email 2: Help Them Understand Their Pain

☑ Email 3: Offer a Pain Solution

Let's go over these in some depth.

Email No.1: Feel Their Pain

As the old sales adage says, you are not selling the hammer. You are selling the hole in the wall.

Every product or service is relieving some kind of pain. That pain could be as simple as:

☑ Wanting a new pool

☑ Wanting a better-tasting pizza

☑ Looking desperately for adequate day-care

☑ The inability to keep roses alive in the front yard

The primary goal of this first email is to...

☑ Establish what the pain point is.

☑ Discuss your own connection to the pain point. ("Believe me, I know how stubborn those damn gophers are!")

☑ Hint that there is a possible solution to this pain.

Note: Do not sell in this email. Do not pitch. You are letting them know you understand.

And the tone here should be emotional, empathetic, understanding. NOT abstract or official!

Email No.2: Help Them Understand Their Pain

This is where you get to flaunt your expert status a bit.

This is where you give them a bit of insight into the BIGGER PICTURE of where their pain point fits in with the grand scheme of things.

In the day-care example, you've already, in Email No.1, talked about the pain of not being able to find quality day-care. (The hectic schedule, the lack of certainty, the anxiety over who to trust.)

Now, you can dig deeper into the problem of adequate day-care. Such as:

☑ No unified certification system

☑ Tough to find honest feedback on providers

☑ Too expensive

☑ No reliable database of names

☑ No monitoring system

You've appealed to their emotion around the pain. Now you've given them a bit of insight and education about the problem. (And made them feel smart in the process, no small thing.)

Now, it's time to move to the solution…

Email No.3: Offer a Solution

This is where you give them the way out of this pain.

This is the day-care membership site, the premier pizza club, the state-of-the-art fiberglass pool, the Golfinator 5000…etc.

Just remember to focus on the benefits, and paint successful word pictures in which they can "see" what it's like to have the product or service.

People don't care about the titanium alloy of the Golfinator 5000 Club. They care about "seeing" their cocky friends look impressed as their golf ball ZOOMS hundreds of yards down the fairway.

Note: Let the video, or sales letter, do the selling. All you want in the email is to tell people to "check out the solution."

How to Sell Stuff and Not Piss People Off

Now you could just send these three emails to your EN-TIRE list.

And that would be (sorta) okay.

If you're offering a low-ticket item that you know everybody might be interested in (such as a 2-for-1 entree deal, then that would be fine.)

But remember, the whole problem with Groupon is they suck at tailoring their offers effectively. (Can't tell you how many emails I get from them offering me deals on facials and chemical peels.)

My personal recommendation would be to create a NEW email list in your autoresponder, focused exclusively on this product offer, and then invite your larger list to opt in to the new list.

This is called List Segmentation. It sounds like a lot of work. (It isn't, and it's super effective.)

Here's how I do it:

- ☑ Write my three emails in the Sales Trinity of Awesomeness.

- ☑ Create a new email list based on the product or service I'm selling, and load up the three-email sequence in that list.

- ☑ Grab the "opt-in code" for that NEW list and create a page on my website where I can send people to sign up for that NEW list.

- ☑ Send an email to my ENTIRE LIST asking if they're interested, and send them to that webpage to opt in.

- ☑ Sit back, and count my money.

Say, I run a golf store. And I've got 1500 people on my list.

And let's say I've got this ultra-awesome golf club that just came in — The Golfinator 5000 — which promises to add forty feet to your drives, and with a picture of a Cobra in flames on the side, promises to make you look like a supreme stud on the greens.

Well, everybody on my list may NOT want a golf club with a cobra on fire. (I know. Crazy, right?)

So, what I would do is: send out an email that said something like:

SUBJ: Ready to Be Awesome?

Hey There Golf Dudes and Dudettes,

Well, we've had an interesting week here.

I might have come across the biggest technological advance in golf that I've seen in the last 20 years.

Now, it may not be for everybody. (It's pretty bold, and could add some serious juice to your drives.)

But again, it's not for everybody.

*So, if you'd like to hear more about it head over here (*Link to Website page with sign-up code for your new email list.*)*

What's the point of this?

Well, you avoid alienating your main email list with offers that they have no interest in.

And so when you promote something else on your email list, whether it's a computer-graphics class or a 24-foot yacht, you'll know you'll be speaking to people who are interested, and motivated by your offers and have the potential to boost your profits enormously.

CHAPTER 6 KEY TAKEAWAYS:

- ☑ We use a three-step email sequence called the Sales Trinity of Awesomeness to sell our products and services.

- ☑ The first email should establish you feel your reader's pain, the second email should help your reader understand their pain, and the third email should give them a solution. (Your product or service.)

- ☑ To avoid email list fatigue, look into list segmentation, in which you create a separate list for that product or service.

Chapter 7:

How to Make Sure Your Emails Get Opened

"It is not enough to conquer, one must learn to seduce."

-Voltaire

Most businesses suck at email marketing.

Want to know how I know?

Though it can fluctuate by market, the average industry standard open rate for email marketing is 10.8%.

You read that right. Nearly 90% of all folks out there don't open the email they get in their inbox.

Now, hopefully you've learned over the course of our email marketing journey together that some techniques can help you stand out from the pack.

But if people never open your email, as they are inclined to do, then all the great initial sequences and sales funnels won't do a bit of good.

So, here are my Top FOUR TIPS to help you get out of the Inbox Slushpile, and into the rarified air of your subscriber's undivided attention.

Tip No.1: Ask Your Subscribers to Add You to the Safe Sender List

This doesn't seem like a big deal, but it is.

Most email clients are as anal as a tax auditor and are looking for any excuse to banish your precious email message to the Siberia of the spam folder. (Especially if you have any "dodgy" words in your subject line or message body.)

The fix is a simple one: just ask your subscribers to "whitelist" you, or add you to the "safe sender" list.

I usually do this in my "welcome" email — the one they get right after they sign up for my email list. And I tell them, straight up, why it's important they do this:

"Hey There. Just a quick reminder Please add my email address to safe sender list. (I want to make sure you get all the cool bonus tips I got for you coming down the pike.")

Even better, you could ask them to "reply" to your email to ensure they got it. (This will ensure all your emails get delivered in their inbox.)

Tip No.2: Write a Kick-Ass Subject Line

Poor open rates can always be traced back to a subject line that either confused, intimidated, or simply bored the reader.

Here are a few down-and-dirty tips when it comes to subject lines:

☑ **Avoid spammy words such as FREE in your subject line.** Readers don't like 'em and the email filters will throw you in the spam folder. A fate far worse than death. (Here's a list of spam words to avoid, from the great folks over at HubSpot - http://punkrockmarketing.com/spam)

☑ **Leave your dictionary at home**. Use conversational words and a conversational tone. (Example: "How Big Bird Ruined My Business" NOT "An Examination of the Many Layered Effects Public Television Has on Consumer Spending.")

☑ **Keep it short.** I mean it. Shoot for under 50 characters. (Most email providers, much like the orchestra at the Academy Awards, will cut you off anyway.)

☑ **Make your subject lines personal, if you can.** (Example: "Oops! Biggest Mistake I Ever Made in Business" NOT "The Mistakes Business Owners Must Avoid.)

☑ **Use specific numbers, not rounded numbers**. This one seems weird. But it totally works. (Example: "How One Pool Cleaner Saved $1,467" NOT "How One Pool Cleaner Saved Over $1,000")

☑ **Make the subject line either TOTALLY WEIRD or TOTALLY focused on a BENEFIT**. Both work, but mediocre stuff in the middle doesn't work so hot. (Example: "I Brought Home a Penguin Today…" AND "The #1 Reason Your Facebook Marketing Sucks" are both subject lines I've used with success.)

TIP NO.3: MAKE YOUR "FROM" NAME PERSONAL

All autoresponders will allow you to customize the FROM email address that subscribers see when they scan your emails.

And unless you're Pepsi or Target or Home Depot — a HUGE brand with INSTANT name recognition — I would advise you to use your name, followed by your company. (Either spelled out or abbreviated.)

So I might do something like:

"FROM: Michael Clarke (Punk Rock Marketing)"

Or…

"FROM: Michael Clarke (PRM)"

If I did use the abbreviation, I would want to let my subscribers know early on what the "PRM" meant. (If I wasn't super clear, somebody might think a political action committee was emailing. Which ain't what I'm going for.)

The point is to get through people's natural distrust of organizations.

Most people scan their inboxes quickly. And they figure emails from "companies" usually involve coupons or offers that they can "get to later." But emails from PEOPLE are different. They may be time-sensitive. There might be important information in there.

There might be something I need to take action on right now. So, make the change and watch your open rates skyrocket.

Tip No.4: Go Easy on the Images

A lot of people check their emails at work, and email clients such as Microsoft Outlook provide the subscriber a snapshot of your email, without them actually having to open the email.

And if your email has got a ton of images, or one large image, then chances are that image will be blocked, until the subscribers click on the "Display images below."

So what's the big deal?

Well, aside from the fact that people are inherently lazy and any single thing that makes it HARDER for them to see your email I'm wholeheartedly against…

…some email clients, such as Outlook, will automatically send emails with photos into the spam folder. (If your subscriber didn't already set up a filter to block image emails.)

Either way, it's an awful lot of risk for the sake of a pretty image.

So, keep the images to a minimum, and small. (Maybe just your logo.) And get to the meat of your email content.

Your open rates, and a grateful (email) nation, will thank you.

CHAPTER 7   KEY TAKEAWAYS:

- ☑ In your welcome email, have new subscribers add you to their "safe senders" list. (Or even better, have them shoot you a quick reply.)
- ☑ Keep your subject lines: short, interesting, personal, non-spammy, specific and conversational.
- ☑ Put your name in the From Address. (Don't just put your company name.)
- ☑ Leave your big images for your website. Hurts open rates.

Chapter 8:

How to Make Sure Your Emails Get Read

"To understand the man, you must first walk a mile in his moccasin."

-North American Indian Proverb

I had a gig once as an A&R guy — you know one of those people who gets paid virtually nothing by a record label to go see a lot of crappy bands, in the hopes of finding the next Nirvana.

I remember on my very first day on the job, probing my boss for some veteran words of wisdom.

Me: "What's the biggest thing I should look for in a band?"

Him: "Short songs about sad things."

I thought he was kidding. He wasn't.

Turns out you can tell a hell of a lot by a band by the length/volatility of a band's repertoire.

That's because everybody's songs are TOO long.

Their intros are too long, their choruses are too long.

And that artful, clever, self-conscious banter in between songs is the longest thing of all.

And the songs would usually have the dumbest, most cliche lyrics; lyrics that even a Celine Dion fan would think was sappy...

But every once in a while I would see a band that got it.

A band who realized songs that got the point quickly, and kept people entertained, and expressed some devastating heartbreak or emotional minefield, was a better way to sell a trunkload of CD's, T-shirts and bumper stickers than any twenty-minute incoherent speech by the lead singer.

"Hit Me Baby, One More Time"

I would contend your emails should be written the same way.

To the point. Personal. And not boring.

Now, I don't believe all your emails have to be a certain length. (Some of my emails can get quite long.)

But I make sure they are NOT boring. (If they are, what's the point of sending them?)

So, here are my Top FIVE Tips for writing compelling emails that get people engaged, interested and willing to listen to what you have to say:

Tip No.1: Bring the Emotion...Fast!

Please don't write:

"In this email I will cover the three challenges most small businesses face…"

But instead…

"Okay, I'll just say it. This economy sucks ass."

Now, you don't have to borrow my liberal use of the English language, but you do need to go for the jugular.

Get to the HEART AND SOUL of the issue. Fast. It's the only way to break through the inbox clutter.

Tip No.2: Tell stories through a main character

When I say "main character," I don't mean you have to write your emails through Hannibal Lecter's perspective. (Although, wouldn't that be cool...)

No, just that people relate to people, and that it's much easier for people to get emotionally invested when you're placing your email message in the covers of a "character."

This can be the subscriber. (In fact, most times it will be.) This can be a former/present customer. This can be you. This can be your business. This can be Donald Trump's hair piece.

If it's a sales-y email, don't just say:

"We have 200 units of the Golfinator 5000 in overstock. Grab yours today."

Make it personal!

"I'm a moron. I ordered too many Golfinators. (They are currently taking up residence in my employee break room.) Help give my employees a place to eat their Lean Cuisine and grab an awesome club today."

If it's a quick tip, don't just say:

"One issue homeowners have is understanding how fiberglass pools are different than other kinds of pools."

Instead...

"Fiberglass gets a bad rap. (Had a customer once tell me he'd rather root for the Dallas Cowboys than put in a fiberglass pool.)

'Well, get your Tony Romo jersey ready,' I told him, because here are a few reasons why fiberglass pools are so awesome..."

Top No.3: Cover Just One (Main) Thing

Ever forget to put something on your to-do list?

And then when you did the task, you put it on your to-do list just so you could cross it off. (I know you have, so don't even pretend.)

That's because us human-types are always looking for small, little areas of our life where we can feel like we're getting stuff done.

And there's nothing more satisfying than cruising through our inbox and getting through the sludge of email that's backed up.

But when a subscriber opens up your email and sees 12 links, 14 paragraphs, three tips and tons of calls-to-action…

…then most subscribers will just delete your email — ie: cross it off their list — then go through the effort of reading your email. (Even if the info is really helpful.)

So, keep your email to one simple concept or idea. (Have three tips for the new homebuyer? Stretch it out over three emails. Have three products you're offering? Send three different emails talking about each one.)

Less is always more when it comes to email marketing.

Tip No.4: Break Up Your Paragraphs

And that less includes the length of your paragraphs.

As you can tell by the way I've organized this book, I like to keep my paragraphs short.

Now, you might find this mortally offensive and against every rule of grammar…

...but, here's the thing, reading words in big blocks of text is hard. (And nobody, except my mother, prints out emails to read.)

I like to keep my paragraphs to about two sentences max. (And I like to throw in plenty of one-sentence, or even one-word, paragraphs.)

TIP NO.5: USE A CLIFFHANGER AT THE END

We touched on this earlier in Chapter 4, where we covered your initial sequence in detail. But let me show you a bit more how it's done.

Basically you want to end every email with a bit of a tease for the next email.

There are many ways to do this:

THE UPFRONT TECHNIQUE

"And you think that's cool? Wait till you see the next email where I show you how to make a 27" HDTV out of chicken wire and old cellphone parts!"

THE "SORRY, I RAN OUT OF ROOM" TECHNIQUE

"Sorry. This email is getting a little long. I'll have to give you my #1 Way to Avoid Federal Taxes tomorrow. But I promise to deliver tomorrow. Scout's honor."

THE "SOAP OPERA ENDING" TECHNIQUE

"And which famous film director said he was going to find me and break my kneecaps? Well, you'll have to tune in tomorrow to find out."

The "Gotta Get Permission Before I Can Tell You" Technique

"And which famous actress is using our skin product to look ten years younger? Well, I can't reveal that. Yet."

"I'll try to do that tomorrow. But I'll give you a hint. (It rhymes with "Peg Dyan.")

CHAPTER 8 Key Takeaways:

☑ Go for an emotional hot button quickly in your email.

☑ Each email should have a main character. Could be you, could be a customer, could be the President of Bulgaria.

☑ Each email should cover one topic. Break up large topics into much smaller topics.

☑ Keep your paragraphs short. Embrace fragments.

☑ End each email with a cliffhanger that teases what will be covered in the next email.

Chapter 9:

5 Secrets to Total World Email Domination

"If people do not believe math is simple, it's because they don't realize how complicated life is."

-John von Neumann

Quick confession: I hate spreadsheets. And Math.

And anything that smells like it came out of a high-school statistics class.

But at some point, even a right-brained English major like me, realizes to be an entrepreneur and avoid having to get some soul-sucking cubicle job…

…my email campaigns have to make a profit.

And the real question isn't about HOW MUCH MONEY you're making.

It's how much money am I willing to spend to acquire new subscribers? (And how can I do it for cheaper than my competition?)

And while there are certainly many ways to lower your Google Pay-Per-Click costs or reduce your Facebook advertising expenses, the REAL way to slash your lead-gen costs is to make your email marketing as kick-ass as possible.

And to do that, you gotta tweak, you gotta test. You gotta

dig into the numbers. (As much as my Shakespeare-lovin' heart disapproves.)

So, what TWEAKS should you make? What should you pay attention to?

Where can you trim the fat, and boost the performance of your email marketing efforts?

Well, here are my FIVE Email Tweaks to Help You Dominate the World and make a lot more profit, without spending more money:

Email Tweak No.1: Remove Your Unsubscribers Every Month

Just because somebody unsubscribed from your email marketing campaign does not mean the autoresponder service has removed them from your list. Most likely they will keep the email address in your database. Which means you continue to pay for that lead.

Get in the habit, every month, of removing every person who unsubscribes from your email list and save yourself money in the process.

Email Tweak No.2: Create New Subject Lines to Boost Open Rates

Oftentimes you'll find, by digging into the reports of your autoresponder, that there's an email or two in your sequence that goes over, as my father used to say, like a "lead fart."

When there's a huge drop in open rates, inevitably it's the subject line.

So, write out a couple of options and try the best ones that don't seem quite as sucky and plug 'em in. (Keep tweaking until you get the open rate back to where you want it.)

EMAIL TWEAK NO.3: SHARPEN CALLS-TO-ACTIONS TO BOOST CLICK-THRU RATES

This will depend, of course, on what you're asking people to click over to.

I'm usually sending people to a sales page that I'm linking to in the bottom of the email. You may be asking people to go to a blog post or a video or a press release.

The key here is to find out which outbound links are working in an email, and which aren't. The only way to do this, with any certainty, is to use analytics. (I know, I hate that word too.)

Google Analytics (http://google.com/analytics) is my weapon of choice. (It's free and fairly easy to use.) And works perfect when you drop in that extra piece of code on the end of a link.

This is absolutely vital when you provide multiple links to the same destination.

Once you get your data you'll want to look at:

- ☑ **Changing the location of the outbound link** by moving it further down the email, or closer to the top.

- ☑ **Changing the Call-to-Action verbiage**. "Click here," "Check Out this Link" or "Download Now" may seem the same to you, but to your subscriber they say very different things.

- ☑ **Changing how the link looks**. Is it "http://yoursite.com/offer" or "http://yoursite.com/?9sf3" or "http://bit.ly/424" or "Click Here Hyperlink"? I prefer pretty URLs, like the first one, but this will require some testing on your part.

- ☑ **Changing how the link is presented**. Is it in bold? Is it in italics? Does it have arrows like this — "==>http://your-site.com<==" — try different variations to see what grabs your email readership.

Email Tweak No.4: Split-Test Your Squeeze Page

All of the traffic in the world won't help if nobody is opting into your list. You should, comfortably, sit at about a 25-35% opt-in rate for your landing page.

If not, refer to Chapter 2 for ideas on how to tweak your landing page. (And if you are above 35%, keep tweaking anyway. You're onto something great.)

But one OTHER way to boost conversions is to split-test two different versions of your squeeze page. (This allows you to show TWO different versions of the same page randomly to web traffic.)

I like to test things such as:

☑ Video vs. Text

☑ Headline #1 vs. Headline #2

☑ Orange "Get Access button" vs. Yellow "Get Access" button. (You think I'm kidding. I'm not. It matters.)

☑ Bullet points vs. No bullet points

☑ More copy vs. Less copy

Again, Google Analytics offers a FREE way to do this with its content experiments service.

You'll have to install Google Analytics on your website — it's a little bit too involved to go into here — but once you do, you just create two different pages on your site and let good old GA do the rest.

Email Tweak No.5: Track Your Sales

This will, of course, depend on what you are, in fact, selling.

If you're selling a simple product online then this will be pretty straightforward and you can track, using Google Analytics, how many people are clicking on a link in your email and eventually reach the "Thank You" page they see when they purchase something.

But if you're a brick-and-mortar business — say, you're a sandwich shop — then you'll need to do something a little more nuanced.

I suggest promoting a coupon, that's only available for your email subscribers, in which they have to either mention some EMAIL CODE WORD or print out the email and bring it to your business.

At the end of each month, you can track your sales percentage against the amount of new leads you get from your email campaign and see how you're doing.

Hopefully, if you follow the techniques we've gone over in this book, you should have a healthy 10-15% conversion rate.

But many marketers make a great living off of a 1-2% conversion rate. (So don't beat yourself up too much if it's low at first.)

CHAPTER 9 KEY TAKEAWAYS:

☑ Tweaking your email campaigns is an easy way to make more money, without increasing your ad spend.

☑ Rewrite any under-performing subject lines to boost open rates. Open rates ALMOST always have to do with subject lines that aren't connecting with readers.

☑ Remove any unsubscribers from your autoresponder database each month. You're paying for them anyway.

☑ Use Google Analytics to track your click-thru rates and split-test your squeeze pages.

☑ Track your sales either through Google Analytics, or with a simple coupon code.

Bonus Chapter:
Thanks, Google, for Ruining Everything

It pains me to write this extra, bonus director's-cut chapter. (Mostly because I had other really important things to do. Like get through my back episodes of "Breaking Bad".)

But then Google went and changed…everything. (And I do mean everything.)

And I didn't feel it was fair to leave you without a tip or two on how to handle this new post-Gmail tab wasteland we find ourselves in.

It might just be the best thing that ever happened to us.

HERE BE MONSTERS (AND A CRAPPY OPEN RATE)

So, in case you have no idea what I'm talking about, Gmail completely changed how it filters emails for its users.

The old interface used to dump all of the email for a subscriber into one single vertical location. (And required its users to filter and organize and figure out how to avoid email overwhelm.)

But then the Google brain trust came up with an idea to divide all email into three tabs: Primary, Social and Promotions.

As a Gmail user, I love it. As a marketer, and somebody who

Because:

- ☑ Gmail will (most likely) deem our broadcast emails as "promotion," even if they aren't. (Unless we take action.)
- ☑ People are lazy and probably won't look at the promotions tab very much. (I know I don't.)
- ☑ Sales will suffer. (Which is bad, bad, bad.)

"I GOT A REMEDY"

So what do we do? Bribe Google? Quit our job? Start an alpaca farm in Pennsylvania?

No.

We take some simple, but super-effective actions that not only can help us survive as marketers in a post-Gmail tab world…

…but actually help us stand out from our competition even further.

So, here are my Top THREE Ninja Tips for Gmail Tab Survival-ness:

GMAIL TAB TIP NO.1: ASK YOUR SUBSCRIBERS TO MAKE YOU A PRIMARY

There are a lot of email marketing gurus who advocate teaching your subscribers to manually "turn off" the Gmail tab organization.

I think that is way overkill. (And frankly a bit unethical. I mean, if they want the tabs, why should you ask them to do something like that?)

But instead, you could film a very quick and short screencast video showing people that by "dragging" your email from the "promotion" tab to the "primary" tab they'll be sure not to miss out on all the great content you'll be sending them.

Add a link to this tutorial video in the welcome message you send to your new subscribers. They'll thank you for the cool way to organize their email and you'll make sure your delivery rates stay high.

Gmail Tab Tip No.2: Ask Your Subscribers to "Reply" to You

This one totally works. (And also helps you look like a really cool person.)

Simply ask your new subscribers in your first email to "reply" to your message. Tell them you want to make sure they got access to the free goodie you're giving away and you want to hear from them if they have any questions about your area of expertise.

Not everybody will reply to you. But A LOT of people will. Once they do, you will automatically be filtered as a primary contact in their inbox.

Best of all: the questions you get from subscribers can give you some great ideas for future content.

Gmail Tab Tip No.3: Do More Social Stuff

If the first two don't seem to help with the whole Gmail tab thing, then ramp up your social media efforts. (Because I have a feeling that the social tab in Gmail will be visited far more than the Promotions tab.)

So, when people sign up for your email list, make sure your Thank You Page has links where they can "Follow you on Facebook" and "Follow Us on Twitter" or "Subscribe to Us on YouTube."

Doing this will help ensure your messages, whether informative or of a marketing nature, get delivered, read and eventually taken action on.

"...AND NOW FOR SOMETHING COMPLETELY DIFFERENT"

I actually think the Gmail tab thing is going to help us. (In the long run.)

Because:

☑ Most of our competitors won't have a clue what to do. (And will abandon email.)

☑ If we tell good "stories" with our email marketing, and we truly send out stuff that helps people, then we have a really good chance at being THE EXPERT in our space.

And when we do that, we have a really good shot at selling way more stuff. (Which is never a bad thing.)

BONUS Key Takeaways:

☑ Don't freak out over the whole Gmail Tab thing. (It's big, but not earth-shattering.)

☑ Record a quick video showing your new subscribers how to add your promotional emails to the Gmail primary tab.

☑ Ask new subscribers to "reply" to your messages to ensure you get looped into the primary list of emails.

☑ Push your new subscribers to follow you on your many social media platforms so you don't miss an opportunity reach your tribe.

Epilogue:
This is Just the Beginning

Hopefully, I've made the case to you that email marketing is more than just weekly newsletter updates.

It's a profound marketing tool that lets business owners cut through all the noise and social media bull-crap that surrounds modern life, and allows you to speak to your subscribers/customers in a personal and meaningful way.

Now, I've misplaced my crystal ball at the moment, so I can't tell you exactly what emails are going to look like in the future. (Will we be able to send video emails? Facebook chats? Twitter feeds? Instagram Mail? Who knows?)

But the core asset of email marketing will never change. Having a list of people you can talk to, over and over again.

I don't know a single marketer or a business person who makes a living EXCLUSIVELY from social media mediums such as Facebook or Twitter. (Unless of course they are selling guides to making a living EXCLUSIVELY from mediums such as Facebook or Twitter.)

I do know plenty of entrepreneurs, myself included, who routinely make serious, living-wage money from just sending out "emails."

And if you stick with this email "thing," you'll do far more than make a lot more money for your business.

You'll hear from thankful subscribers who feel like you wrote that email message "just for them."

You'll get handwritten thank you notes and home-baked

cookies sent to your house as appreciation for what you do.

You'll find people asking your opinion about a myriad of subjects, because they see you as an "expert" in your field.

And no matter what marketing tool or social media platform comes along in the future, solving people's problems and understanding their pain will never go out of style.

*   *   *

~FREE GOOD STUFF~

Exasperated over email? Hit delete on that emotion!

To grab your very own FREE Email Marketing Cheat Sheet, head over to **PunkRockMarketing.com** TODAY and get instant access to your very own Email marketing checklist.

It's so easy, Russian hackers can do it without sending you a virus!

Again, head over to PunkRockMarketing.com TODAY and get your FREE Email Marketing Cheat Sheet.

And if you have any questions, just drop me a line at Michael@punkrockmarketing.com.

"Regrets, I've Had a Few..."

By the time I finish typing this sentence...

...There will be a BRAND-NEW social network that you and I absolutely HAVE to drop everything we're doing and sign up for.

It'll be called "Social Zoom" or "FriendyBot" or "BluMeanie." And everyone you know — and don't know — will tell you the only way to market your wares in the 21st century is by spending 17 hours a day "posting" or "sharing" or "zweeping" on these must-have social platforms.

Or even worse, the strategies and techniques and methodologies I've outlined in this humble tome will become horribly — and painfully — outdated by the time I hit "publish."

Facebook will suddenly decide, without warning, that all Fan Page owners MUST not only "pay" for their content to be seen, but they must also get a "I (Heart) Mark Zuckerberg" neck tattoo to boost the visibility of their status updates.

Twitter, in the future, may feel 140 characters is far too verbose for its users, and require that all tweets contain no more than 20 characters, and be written in one-word sentences. ("Here. Coupon. Buy. RT.")

And posting a 12-second video on YouTube may force you to take a blood oath of allegiance to the Cult of Google. ("I hereby swear, to never turn ON my Gmail privacy settings...")

But...

...whether the tools and platforms outlined in this book change — and they will change, trust me — the big-picture strategies we've gone over will NOT change.

In my never-humble opinion, we've reached a point of no return.

Boring, old, business-as-usual marketing — "Here's my thing! Buy it now!" — just doesn't work anymore. (If it ever did.)

Consumers don't want anything that has the "whiff" of marketing. More than deals, offers, sales and coupons, they want… a story.

They want the buying experience to be, just that, an experience.

They want to be able to tell their friends about that cool, handcraft jewelry maker they found on Facebook and bought a necklace from.

They want to blab about that artisan pizza joint — run by those whacky hippies from Vermont — who send out those funny email newsletters.

They want to recount the time they won a video contest on Pinterest, which got them the 60-minute coaching call that changed their life.

And the more we can keep things visual, fun, interactive — and give our customers plenty of opportunities to be recognized and feel "wicked smaht" — then no matter what social media platform comes down the pike…

…we'll be in a position to crush anything our competition — and those pesky big-box retailers — can throw at us.

Here's hoping this book has given you a strategy or two to begin your quest for world (marketing) domination.

Talk soon,

Michael Clarke
PunkRockMarketing.com
Michael@punkrockmarketing.com
Twitter: @punkrockbiz
Facebook.com/PunkRockMarketing

www.ingramcontent.com/pod-product-compliance
Lightning Source LLC
Chambersburg PA
CBHW052143070326
40689CB00051B/3182